You Just

Wouldn't Believe It

You Just
Wouldn't Believe It

From Reactive to
Creative Leadership

Daniel Ofman
Guust Verpaalen

servire

Servire: nieuwe wegen naar wijsheid, inspiratie en spiritualiteit

www.servire.nl/be
www.boekenwereld.com

Published by Servire, a division of Kosmos-Z&K Uitgevers, Utrecht/Antwerpen

© 2006 Text and Illustrations by the Authors and Kosmos-Z&K Uitgevers, Utrecht/Antwerpen
Cover design: Jos Peters, Huizen
Layout and design of Text and Illustrations: Punten & Komma's, Utrecht

ISBN-10: 90 215 8216 3
ISBN-13: 978 90 215 8216 0
D/2006/0108/189
NUR 801

TABLE OF CONTENTS

MY LIFE IN FIVE BRIEF CHAPTERS[1]

1) I walk down a street.
   There is a deep hole in the sidewalk.
   I fall in.
   I am lost, I am helpless.
   It isn't my fault.
   It takes forever to find a way out.

2) I walk down the same street.
   There is a deep hole in the sidewalk.
   I pretend I don't see it.
   I fall in again.
   I can't believe I'm in the same place.
   But it isn't my fault.
   It still takes a long time before I'm out of it.

3) I walk down the same street.
   There is a deep hole in the sidewalk.
   I see it is there.
   I fall in again… it's a habit.
   My eyes are open.
   I know where I am.
   It's my fault.
   I get out immediately.

4) I walk down the same street.
   There is a deep hole in the sidewalk.
   I walk around it.

5) I walk down a different street.

---

[1] Portia Nelson. In *The Tibetan Book of Living and Dying*, Sogyal Rinpoche, Cothen 1994

DIALOGUE

Guust: You wouldn't believe it!
Daniel: You wouldn't believe what?

Guust: It!
Daniel: What do you mean, "it"?

Guust: The "it" of "It, we and I."
Daniel: Oh, that "it." Why didn't you say so in the first place?!

Guust: Yep, that "it"! Do you understand it now?
Daniel: What it?

Guust: Oh, put a sock in it! It's not important.
Daniel: It's not important? I thought you just said it was?

Guust: Well, it is, but you just don't understand it.
Daniel: What don't I understand?

Guust: It!
Daniel: What "it" are you talking about now?

Guust: Look, I'll spell it out for you. Imagine that you're walking along the beach and…
Daniel: The sun sets… you just wouldn't believe it!
Guust: Oh, let's start again, shall we?

1 A NEW CHALLENGE FOR DANIEL

There was once a factory which employed 2,000 people. It produced a product that has a damaging effect on people's health, namely cigarettes. The business did not exactly have a glowing reputation, nor was it one to mention with pride over a birthday party drink because you knew you could expect a volley of cynical reactions. Not only can smoking damage your health; you can also die from it. That is what it says on the packet, and there is no doubt about it. As such, you would be better off not smoking. Despite this, there are 1.5 billion smokers in the world.

The statistics showed that the business was not doing badly. Its market share was on the up and up, and productivity and profits had been increasing for years on end. This factory alone produced nearly 100 billion cigarettes per year, again an increase over the past years. The business was under no threat at all and there was no crisis looming. It had become accustomed to growth and to its recent successes.

Its management team held an annual business retreat somewhere in the country (a common thing for management teams to do). They would rehash everything: where they were doing well, where there was room for improvement, what they should focus on in the immediate future, what their corporate mission and vision was, what strategies and goals were to be pursued, and so on. Every self-respecting management team posed questions like this, and this cigarette manufacturer was no exception.

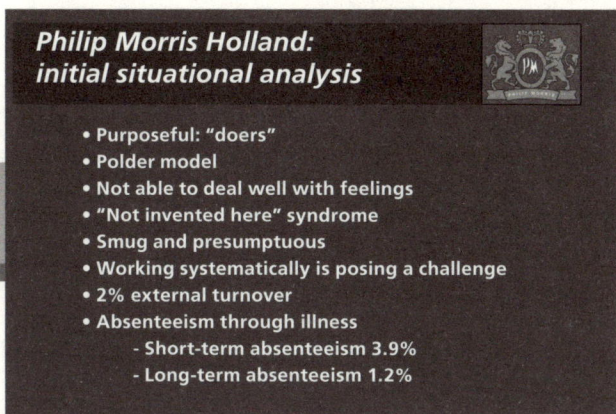

Philip Morris Holland:
initial situational analysis

- Purposeful: "doers"
- Polder model
- Not able to deal well with feelings
- "Not invented here" syndrome
- Smug and presumptuous
- Working systematically is posing a challenge
- 2% external turnover
- Absenteeism through illness
    - Short-term absenteeism 3.9%
    - Long-term absenteeism 1.2%

This figure shows some of the issues that were on the list of strengths and weaknesses.

"Not able to deal well with feelings" was by no means a new issue. It was a regular item on the annual strengths and weaknesses analysis, and it was no wonder, since 90% of the team was male. However, this time a new Human Resources Manager made a somewhat out-of-the-ordinary comment: "Either we do something about it now or we shelve the topic entirely." Since it was hardly fitting to pass the issue off as irrelevant (as had been done in the past), a pilot training course was organized. And so it happened that I (Daniel) was invited by the Human Resources Manager to familiarize myself with the business with a view to investigating this issue. At this stage I was still connected with Kern Konsult. Later I set up a new consultancy: Core Quality (www.corequality.nl). My name was mentioned simply because the Human Resources Manager had only recently been employed by this business, and during his term with his previous employer had employed me to implement an extensive training course for managerial staff. So we renewed our acquaintance, but within a completely different environment.

My first impressions were not very encouraging. The issue I had to investigate had something odd about it and in view of the product itself and the company's image (which I was familiar with through the press and other media), I had serious doubts about whether I wanted to work for the cigarette company. To add to this, the Human Resources Manager told me immediately that the fastest way to get everybody's back up was to ask people not to smoke during a meeting. I had intended to do this.

The fact that it was a pilot program also aroused my suspicions. Pilot programs are on occasion used to quietly bury an issue that cannot be avoided, but that is not really taken seriously. You will have given it your attention, but thankfully nothing has come of it. I had previous experience of this sort of thing and did not wish to repeat it. You are, in fact, being used: there are other agendas at work.

In short, there were reasons aplenty for declining the assignment, particularly since some of my colleagues had immediately indicated that they were not interested in going along with it.

Nevertheless, there was something that intrigued me. Looking at a business from the sidelines and condemning it is easy. For many years, I had been aware that my value judgments derive from two sources: sources which are independent of each other and should be kept that way. The first are the things that I have a negative reaction to – that I am "allergic to". The second are my personal values.

For years I have been saying out loud that you can learn the most from people with whom you have the greatest difficulty, because they form part of your personal challenge. This is what you can detect so clearly in the core quadrants. And, as you will have gathered, the company triggered a strong initial repugnance in me. Running away because I felt so strongly about it would mean missing an opportunity to learn more about myself.

But another mechanism that triggers my value judgments is my values being put under attack. As soon as anybody starts trampling on my personal values, I have a tendency to distance myself and want to have nothing more to do with that person or that organization. Living with values means that I have certain boundaries, and hence it is understandable that I make value judgments. The challenge for me is not to let my value judgments degenerate into prejudices. The fact that this company aroused value judgments in me, put me on guard and made me want to investigate where these had come from. I became aware that my value judgments were based on prejudices and disapproval deriving from others, and not from my own experiences. It made taking on the company's assignment increasingly interesting. I ended up becoming really keen to investigate what the underlying issue was and whether I could contribute towards it. Ultimately, I wanted to form an opinion, but not condemn.

Now, years later, I can say without equivocation that I am delighted that I investigated the underlying issue behind the at first sight singular question of how to deal better with our feelings.

The process that followed was one of the most inspiring courses of development that I have been privileged to take part in. Why? Because it was real, serious and sincere, and because it touched on the very nature of leadership. Because it worked, bore fruit, could be gauged. Because it generated energy both within the organization and in those in charge of the process, and because it was directed at lasting results and not at short-term effects. It was an inspiring time, a quest full of uncertainty and doubt. It was exciting, full of adventure and based on mutual respect, and it was open and honest.

During its course, I got to know Guust as a manager and leader, but most of all as a person and a friend. It was like a breath of fresh air to meet someone who was prepared to show his vulnerability and to base his leadership not on externals and status but on his inner conviction, vision and courage. This is something that I do not encounter often.

How do you get a developmental process directed at an organization underway when it is a company with 2,000 employees? Where do you focus? What do you do? How do you go about it? And above all, what is your goal? It was a process that took five years of hard work. It was full of rich experiences: experiences so rich that when we looked back on it we both felt the need to write down what had actually happened. Too much had happened (often as a result of acting on an intuitive basis) to ignore. What could we learn from it? What would we do differently the next time? What did we actually do? What worked well and what did not? The real problem was that a retrospective evaluation depends on having a clear organizational framework – and we did not have such a thing. We had not drawn up a prior staged plan of action. The entire process had a highly organic nature. One of its characteristics was that we believed that if we made a move, the next step would manifest itself. And this is what happened. Nevertheless, we did have an implicit model that we let ourselves be guided by. It was a simple one involving the "it" side of the organization (systems and structures), the "we" side (culture and environment), and the "I" side (leadership and responsibility).

In retrospect, we seem to have let ourselves be guided far more by this model than we thought at the time. It would also seem that the model is a much more fundamental one than we ever realized. It has enabled us to see why intervening in one particular way or taking a certain course of action did work while other ways did not. We can now see the many valuable leads the model offers and how it can be put to practical use. In short, it helps us see why we did the things that we did intuitively. The result is that the model has taken on a greater depth of meaning: one that we would like to share with the reader.

Originally, we wanted to make a time journey and describe the five-year process chronologically: this is what we did first and then that, and when that was shown to work, what the next step was, and so on. We eventually decided to link our experiences more to the new model that we had discovered along the way and to illustrate it with some anecdotes. A description of the process in chronological terms has been included in Part III: what the model is made up of.

The working title that we started out with was *It Lacks Credibility*, and, like so much of the process, the title came out of the blue during the course of the project. If there is anything that is clearer than ever, it is that a lot of the traditional organizational approaches work to only a limited extent, because the assumptions that form the basis of them are not credible. Inferences that relate to financial analyses are flawed inferences if they are based on rational considerations alone.

For some time the working title was *Inspiration is the Key*; another one was *Inspiration Deciphered*, by which we meant that when you learn to see that some things are just not true or credible, you uncover vital forces: forces that you can decipher and which have been freed from the world of facts and figures. It is often facts and figures and the desire to express everything in that form that causes us to lose contact with our source of inspiration: our vital forces. We opted for the first of these two titles because we have seen that vital forces – the passions that move individuals – are able to take away the overwhelming power of facts and figures to determine organizations. Without a source of inspiration, an organization will die under the weight of its facts and figures; with it, they will be able to acquire the supportive function that they are capable of having.

When we had finished writing our account and read through it one last time, we ended up opting for the title *You Just Wouldn't Believe It!*, by which we wanted to cast doubt on our tendency to believe that, if we have finally put some order into the "it" side of an organization (its systems and structures), everything will be in order. Our experiences have shown that this is not the case. This book is a plea to take a more balanced view of organizations, an approach in which values, culture, personal responsibility, inspiration and creativity are given the same value as facts and figures, goals and plans. We wanted the subtitle *From Reactive to Creative Leadership* to emphasize the crucial role of leadership. *Bezieling en Kwaliteit in Organisaties* [*Core Qualities: a Gateway to Human Resources*[1]] published in 1992, introduced a number of organizational models. In *Kernachtig* (2001), I described how we applied these models to our own consultancy. This book is about applying these inspiring ideas to a large multinational company.

To clarify this, the next chapter contains a short description of the model that we started out with. Next we deal with the new model: the model that we refined on the basis of our retrospective view. After that, we will give a few examples of how it has worked in practice.

But first of all, let us go back to the beginning.

---

[1] Daniel Ofman, *Core Qualities: a Gateway to Human Resources*. Published by Scriptum Publishers, ISBN 90 5594 240 5.
[2] Daniel Ofman, *The Core Qualities of the Enneagram*, Published by Scriptum Publishers, ISBN 90 5594 208 X.

A NEW CHALLENGE FOR GUUST 2

When I moved from the Government Accounting Service to Philip Morris Holland in Bergen op Zoom in 1985, I had no idea of the opportunities that this American cigarette manufacturer would have in store for me. At that stage, it was one of the largest employers in the province of Brabant, but one with a somewhat dubious reputation. This was not due to the fact that we manufactured cigarettes: at that time this was a very minor social issue. Its reputation had more to do with a social conflict in the factory two years prior to that date: a conflict which culminated in a strike that had left deep traces not only within the organization but also outside it. I still vividly remember being regularly asked why I was going to work there, of all places. I am still happy that I did take up the challenge to set up an internal accounting service within Philip Morris Holland. The opportunities that the company offered I accepted eagerly. After I had filled various financial positions, I was invited to work at the European headquarters in Lausanne. This wonderful experience of working in a foreign country culminated several years later in my appointment as Financial Director back in Bergen op Zoom. A mere nine months later, however, I was asked whether I would like to become the Manufacturing Director. Despite my total astonishment, I immediately said yes. It was a purely instinctive decision: things of a technical nature were hardly in my line. I could barely hang a painting on a wall in my home. But right from the beginning of my career, I had had an interest in processes and the role of the individual in them. I instinctively felt that I could extend that interest by taking on the role that was being offered to me.

I have always found facts and figures less interesting than the world beyond them: only logical, in view of my Enneagram type: "the Observer". I learned to look on from a very early age: as the only child of parents who ran a pub, I spent my early years taking in all the various customers. Many publicans develop a fine instinct for people. My father also had a very good feeling for business and was particularly known as a person who did honest business (my mother often complained that he was too honest for his own good): my main legacy from him and from my hardworking mother was a sense of justice and fair play. Alongside my intense curiosity, this sense has developed into one of my core qualities. It was with these qualities, plus a good analytical ability provided by my educational training, that I set out on the adventure of directing the Manufacturing Department of the biggest Philip Morris factory outside America.

Right from the very start I was struck by the fact that the individual employee, despite making the product and being responsible for quality and efficiency, was not seen as the main factor in the manufacturing process. Faster machines and better computerization were what it was all about: the employees had to do their best to keep up. As far as the business was concerned, there was not a cloud on the horizon. There had been a lot of investment and the business had grown massively. Our social image had been polished up. We were known for being a socially oriented company, one that looked after its employees. Indeed, it could almost be described as a corporate culture that spoiled its employees.

But things were changing in the world outside. The product itself was starting to become the subject of fierce debate. Further afield, new competitors were making their presence felt: factories in countries whose salary costs were considerably lower than ours. I spent quite a number of hours talking about a change in corporate culture with Dany Cruysberghs, who was Human Resources Director in the same period. We both agreed that it was necessary. It was very apparent to us that the time had come to take a new direction. A change in corporate culture was desperately needed. But how do you go about changing an organization that many regarded as being the very model of an internationally successful business? We did have another option, namely to exploit the situation as best as we could without really initiating a process of change, and then to hope to get a timely promotion that would remove us from the scene. It would then be up to the person who inherited the situation to find a way of dealing with it. This happens all too often, unfortunately. I am a firm believer in accepting the consequences of your own actions right from the moment that you find yourself in such situations. How long should you be prepared to do this? In my opinion, for a period of five years at least. I am convinced that many a manager or director would make quite different decisions if they realized that they would have to deal with the consequences of their own decisions. However, there is a tendency within society to focus on the very short term, particularly where career planning is concerned. The faster the promotion the better. The reverse is also true: it is not wise to stay in the same position for too long, because it can become too routine after a period of time. Then the "I've seen it all" syndrome can overcome you, causing the essential quality of alertness and interest in internal processes to change into a certain apathy and lack of desire to initiate change.

Let us return to Philip Morris. I opted for a process of structural change, but I did not yet know how I would go about it. It was at about the same time that a pilot study started with Daniel and his consultancy: a course in leadership, which would involve a number of people in managerial positions being confronted with questions about how they were functioning, what their ambitions and qualities were, where the pitfalls lay, what the challenges were and what things were rubbing them up the wrong way.

It was no standard course. This quickly became apparent to me from the sometimes unpredictable reactions on the part of the participants. I was curious enough to want to investigate, together with Dany, what was going on. After I was appointed General Director, we – Daniel,

Dany and I – embarked energetically on a unique developmental project. Its guiding principles corresponded very closely to my ideal image of how an organization should work. As I see it, the best results are always obtained when people go to work with pleasure, do their work with pleasure, and return home with pleasure. It sounds simple but how could it be realized in an organization whose employees numbered nearly 2,000?

People (and therefore organizations) often change most quickly when disaster or some other threat is looming. As an industry, we were, of course, acquainted with hard times, though these were always at a remove from the realities of the shop floor. And after all, production had increased every year, so why should anything change? It is like it is with human beings: it is only when you get sick that you are prepared to change your lifestyle. I wanted to avoid such a situation arising in the first place. The answer was simple: we needed to work on a change of consciousness. There was nothing wrong with the company's structures and systems. I would even go so far as to say that, like many companies, these played the dominant role and thus could have a strangling effect. It was at the individual level that there had to be some change, since there can only be a change in corporate culture if individuals change. This also meant paying attention to change at the managerial level: after all, all eyes would be on us to see if we ourselves were prepared to change as well.

I am still working on my own personal development. For me, a two-day course or a seminar is not the way. I would say I spend about fifteen days a year on personal development and self-reflection, but doing it in solitude. I peel off one layer of the onion at a time. I am nowhere near reaching the center and so I hope my life will be a long one. You have to dare to look into yourself, if you want to implement a similar process within your organization.

I do not think that there is an infallible recipe for going about change, or a set of steps that you can just follow one-by-one. You just have to try it out for yourself. Start with the personal development of the managerial staff, because they are the ones who are most troubled by their all-too-visible egos. The corporate culture will automatically start to change at that moment. Once you get underway, the next step will spontaneously manifest itself, or at least so it seemed to me. However, this will only happen as long as you remain alert to what is going on around you and are prepared to view the facts and figures in conjunction with what you glean from others' experiences and your own emotions. The most important lesson that I can teach anyone is to always seek involvement, always seek integration and never to polarize.

Our collaboration with Core Quality (or Kern Konsult, as it was known then) and with Daniel in particular, was of inestimable value. Later, when working on this book, I became more aware that we had in fact followed a certain system. It was certainly not perfect. A lot of things could have been done better.

I have not been able to include all our stories in this book, but have opted for a number of experiences written from my perception of what happened. Only the names of those involved have been changed.

I am indebted to a lot of colleagues within the company. I will make an exception here and mention two of them by their real names. In the first place, Dany Cruysbergh, a co-initiator right from the start: without him as inspiration and good friend, the process would probably not have got underway at all.

The second name that I would like to mention is that of one of my heroes, Wilma Klesman, because of her courage to face life following a tragic incident and her deep-seated sense of values. The following text was written by her:

Richness is
A flower that blooms and I am privileged to see it,
Stars in the heavens that seem only to shine for me,
Friendship given without anything being asked in return.

These are the things that money cannot buy.
The things that make us millionaires.
Would I want anything else?

I was recently asked to move to Marketing and Sales. The experience that we describe in this book in the light of our model has to do with the merger of our two Benelux offices.

At present, in my capacity as Area Vice-President of Northern Europe I am privileged to be putting into practice the model that Daniel and I described. It pleases me to be able to apply it to the many issues that we as cigarette manufacturers are confronted with. I am convinced that doing so will bring Philip Morris closer to socially responsible entrepreneurship than many (both inside and outside the company) now realize.

PART I
THE MODEL

3 THE TRIANGULAR DEVELOPMENTAL MODEL

The original developmental model for organizations was based on a triangle: there was the "it" side, the "we" side and the "I" side. During the 1980s, when the notion of quality was the "in" theme amongst managers, I had already become aware of the fact that processes relating to the development of organizations can be looked at from various perspectives. The organization "New Style Management and Work" (*Management en Arbeid Nieuwe Stijl* or *MANS*) was forthright in its advocacy of the structural approach to improving quality, particularly in Dutch industry. It was a typically rational and data-based approach, directed towards making work processes measurable. The catch-cry of the moment was "measure and know", and all attention was directed towards Quality Control programs. The idea that the work climate was also important was certainly around, but where it fitted into the approach was unclear. The premise was that as long as you could "communicate", you would manage. It was during that period that I realized that there were at least three sides to the matter: the "it", "we" and "I" sides.

The "it" side is the most impersonal side. To activate the "it" side of an organization is to work within "the System": its procedures, regulations, structures and primary work processes. Here, the basic principle is "measure and know": basing decisions more on facts and less on opinions. If you said "Things always go wrong here", you would be asked first of all "What do you mean by 'things', how often is 'always', and where is 'here'?". This is the domain of management techniques: its tools. Systems are analyzed and optimized using logical, rational and linear thought processes. Cause and effect analyses, Pareto analyses, strengths and weaknesses analyses, trend analyses, and viability analyses are only some of the methods that one can resort to. A project based on obtaining Quality Care certification is one example of an approach that focuses on the "it" side of the organization. You describe what it is that you do and you lay it down in the form of regulations and procedures. "It" then improves and the organizational process becomes more reliable, more predictable and easier to control. The eventual result is better quality. This is how manufacturing businesses and the service sector go about systematic improvement. Many organizations want more "tools" like these: more techniques, a more effective structure and more knowledge. "The more I know, the better the solution" is the idea behind this solution-finding type of thinking. Interest in project-based approaches, for example, derives from the desire to use more effective work methods to achieve results. Analysis, structure, phasing and control are the magic words. Most management courses deal with the "it" side: looking for solutions that are about systems and structures.

As one top manager once put it, increasing the supply of tools and instruments will only result in an escalation of violence of the intellectual sort: you could even compare it to an escalating arms race.

And why would you want to do so, when you have other options available?

You could start with the "we" side, for example. This would mean working on the climate for working together, on the organizational culture, on teamwork and on identity. This would mean paying attention to the things that connect people. Good systems and procedures only work if people want them to work and can make them work. If the organizational climate is such that people are tripping each other up whenever they get the chance, then better systems or tools will only be used to attack each other with renewed force. The problems are more likely to have been caused by the corporate culture – the customs and ingrained habits that have developed within the company – than by the company's structures or systems. Having an insight into how corporate cultures operate is a precondition for any manager wanting to direct developmental processes.

Working on the "we" side also means developing the skills needed to create an open climate in which creativity can blossom. This is why tools that have a positive effect on the "it" side (such as cause and effect analyses) only have a limited effect. The nature of the problem is different and so finding solutions will require a different work approach.

Then there is the "I" side. This is the side of personal initiative, of individual will and of taking on the responsibility of making choices and acting creatively instead of reactively. It needs inspired and enthusiastic leadership based on self-knowledge and insight into one's own core qualities. Ultimately, it is about every individual within the organization making choices that are founded on common interest and rapport. The "I" side could also be called the inner dimension of the developmental process. It is not about techniques or skills, but about developing awareness, feeling, passion and zeal.

This triangular model has been particularly useful in detecting the best way of initiating the first stage of a developmental process. In a corporate culture that is focused on taking very active approaches, the "it" side could be addressed first. An effective way of approaching a corporate culture which is under no external threat is often via the culture itself, while an "I" side approach may catch on where there is a lot of tension or unresolved hurt.

We did not draw up a staged plan of action for the developmental process. Organizational development is a process in which you have to browse around: those in charge of it could count themselves lucky to be a step ahead. Sometimes it meant going along with what is expected; sometimes it was useful to do the opposite: something that was absolutely unexpected. The approach will depend largely on what management wants and has opted for.

The triangular approach is a useful concept in its own right, one which for years has helped me to detect those issues that developmental processes need to address. You could describe the concept as a set of areas that require particular attention. Problems will almost always occur in the form of "it", "we" or "I" problems, and as such it is useful to be able to make a distinction between them. What I did not realize for a long time was that not only do they represent a useful way to approach development, but that they are fundamentally different forms of reality and stand for worlds of their own. Not only that, but these worlds seem unable to tolerate each other or would prefer to exclude each other.

What the triangular approach ("it"-"we"-"I") did was raise the issue of where to focus our attention. This was a good approach, and meant that the focus would sometimes be on culture ("we"), sometimes on leadership ("I") and sometimes on plans and objectives ("it"). We would then improvise enthusiastically on the idea (and what happened at Philip Morris Holland was no exception). However, the result did not always come up to expectations. Why not?

The conclusion that Guust and I came to after evaluating five years of work within Philip Morris was that the results were disappointing if we only stuck to working on themes from one particular point of view. In other words, if you only worked on systems and structures from the "it" perspective, you would be limited in the way you could deal with the theme. The same applied to approaching leadership from the "I" perspective: it would be a one-sided approach. We would also find ourselves stranded if we only worked on corporate culture from the "we" perspective, just as we would if we only worked on efficiency from the "it" perspective.

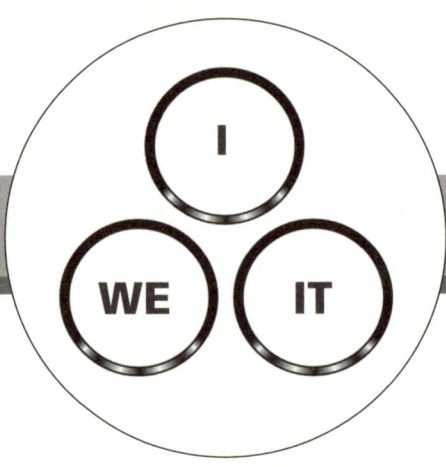

Our approach just did not work if we operated on the assumption that we could achieve lasting results in "it" terms without including the "we" and "I" perspectives. In short, there was something wrong with our model. Looked at in visual terms, what it came down to was that the model was not so much one with three sides as one with three focal points.

THE TRIFOCAL DEVELOPMENTAL MODEL 4

Ken Wilber's book, *The Marriage of Sense and Soul*[3], encouraged a deepening of insight into this model. In this brilliantly written book, Wilber deals in depth with the fundamental differences between the three types of reality and the necessity to integrate them. He makes use of the same terms "it", "we" and "I", but assigns to them a depth that changed our triangular model into the trifocal model.

The crucial issue here is the extent to which the lenses overlap. As we see it, lasting results cannot possibly be achieved by working on only one of the three. In this book, we hope to show that this approach has far-reaching consequences for how an organization is managed.

---

[3] *The Marriage of Sense and Soul*, Ken Wilber, Gateway, ISBN 0 7171 3235 8.

Ideally, the overlap between the three circles should be as great as possible. To put it another way, it is only when the three circles or focal points (representing the way you see the world) overlap that you can see through them simultaneously. The point is that all three different realities are true. If you only look through one of them you deny the reality of the other two, and so what you see is an illusion. Only the center has any depth and that is the only position from which you can see reality. The fact that you do not want to see the other realities does not mean that they are not there. What, then, do they look like?

If you look more deeply into the division of "I", "we" and "it" it will become apparent that what we are dealing with is three "value spheres", as Wilbur calls them, namely art, morals and science. In their time, the Greeks called them "the Beautiful, the Good and the True". In my view, these three words themselves give a completely new nuance to the three that we have already mentioned.

What is True?
What is Good?
What is Beautiful?

As we see it, if this book had no effect other than to raise these three quintessential questions every time an issue needed to be resolved in "Management land", this would be enough to bring about more effective and decisive decision-making.

The True or "it" lens

As a rule, the True is about objective reality and is synonymous with the "it" side. It is the domain of empirical knowledge. From a scientific point of view, a thing is real if it can be observed and reproduced. This is the world of facts and figures, of "measure and know", a world that can be grasped, that is predictable, reproducible, reliable and controllable. It is about exposing the objective truth, which is something different from my personal truths.

This world is a digital one: it is true or not true, a one or a zero. It enables us to get a grasp on things, since we assume that if we can measure things, we will know where we are and can get matters under control. The desire to make things objective can help us in major ways. If our thoughts are confused by opinions, assumptions, fantasies and coloured feelings, objective facts can show us the way and prevent us from making the wrong decisions. Gravity is a reality, and if we jump off a cliff there is no doubt that a painful death will await us. There is no denying such facts, and their reality is not the reality of personal conviction. It is useful to know this if you want to survive.

If we have such a perspective, we are inclined to classify everything that cannot be measured as irrelevant and everything that cannot be controlled as a threat. We need to avoid doing this.

Empirical science's claim that it has a monopoly on the truth is, however, unjustified. It is just not true. It has no credibility (or at least, you would be wise not to believe it). Things that cannot be objectively measured (often branded as superstition), are often simply brushed aside as not being of much concern. Science is not interested in subjectivity, nor in individuality, simply because they are not part of its vocabulary.

The language in which objective reality is couched is the "it" form: the impersonal third person form. The way it describes reality takes the form of a monologue. By this we mean speaking *at* one another, without any interaction. Empirical science seeks research subjects that do not talk back. Fortunately, there is never any need to contradict cogs, light bulbs, research findings and end-of-financial-year reports. You do not have to talk to a molecule in order to describe its properties. Or so we thought for a long time. But although quantum physics is making it increasingly obvious that it is no longer tenable to look at science like this[1], in everyday life we still assume that a fact is a fact: that there is such a thing as data that is objective and has no connection with the observer. What a fine thing it would be if managers in particular heeded the words of Niels Bohr when he said, "If quantum mechanics hasn't shocked you, you haven't understood it yet."

Managers in training learn the language of "it" in business management courses: the language of facts and figures, targets, results and so on. If it is the only language they learn, they will not become acquain-

---

[1] *What tHe βLεεp Dθ ωΣ (k)πow!?* , William Arntz, Betsy Chasse, Mark Vincente. Harper Collins, ISBN 07 5730 334X.

ted with the world of "we" and "I", let alone to integrate them. This will seriously handicap the manager, actually making him unable to represent things clearly, to have well-informed opinions and to make the right decisions: "it" without "we" and "I" is a fiction, and hence has no credibility.

The Good or "we" lens

The Good is about how you and I deal with each other, about interaction, dialogue and ethics. Seen from the "we" perspective, common values are the main thing. Freedom, equality and justice are the pillars on which we have built our society over the course of time: they form the very basis of our living together within that society.

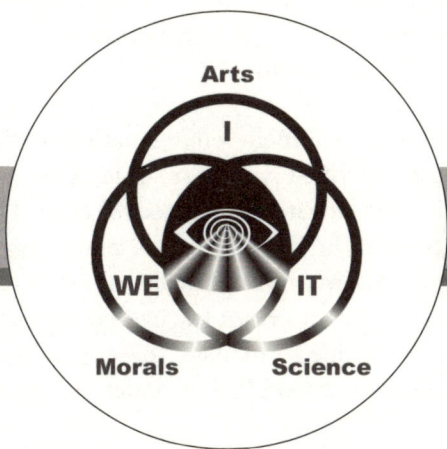

Without shared values, communities of every kind (including organizations) fall apart. This is not to say that we have to interpret freedom, equality and justice in the same way. It does mean that we need to talk about how we view them. How can we live in decency with each other and with every other living thing? Not being in dialogue with each other leads to war. Dialogue means being in conversation with somebody, attempting to understand that person instead of talking at him or her in order to bring him or her over to your point of view (which would be a monologue). "It"-oriented managers talk *at* human objects (a monologue), while "we"-oriented managers talk *with* their fellow man (a dialogue).

Goodness is what a "we" perspective strives for. Without common values, we are no more than a group of individuals gone astray or rampant cancer cells within the organism that we call Earth.

History teems with examples of behaviour that is destructive because of a lack of common human values.

How we deal with each other in organizational contexts and how we choose to interpret "goodness" is consequently equally important. It will determine our behaviour. The way we do business with our co-workers, shareholders, clients and suppliers is what gives our corporate culture its particular colour.

Ecology, care of the environment, emancipation, socially responsible entrepreneurship and ethical issues are some of the broad issues that justify an organization's existence. Correct or ethical behaviour has a language all of its own: the "we" language, a language which uses the "we" form. Anyone in a managerial position has to learn that language. If it has not been learnt or not learnt well enough, the person in question will never be able to manage three focal points simultaneously and see the depth of field this provides, let alone integrate "it", "we" and "I".

The Beautiful or the "I" lens
"Beauty is in the eye of the beholder" is a well-known saying. By it we mean that beauty is an individual experience (an "I" experience) and is largely a subjective one. Facts do not have to play a part in such an experience by any means: it derives from the human ability to discern quality from lack of it. This discerning ability makes it possible for the individual to recognize beauty and experience fulfilment, to live it to the full and to bring it to expression.

The world seen through the "I" lens is an inner world. The things you experience as having value and providing satisfaction may be subjective and consequently not scientifically relevant, but the fact that science has never proved that our spirit exists is not to say that it does not. To know that it does, you only have to close your eyes and direct your attention inward. Then you really do know that there is an inner world. This inner world is also real, only of a different reality to the objective reality that you see via the "it" lens.

Seen from the "I" perspective, the inner world and self-understanding are all-important. The world that you have within you is the only one that matters. This is why "know thyself" is such an important motto. Whatever happens is liable to be interpreted in various subjective ways and the reality I observe is always a co-creation: one of which I am part. I am unable to observe the world objectively because my world is coloured by who I am, by my capabilities, by my own soul forces and my feeling world.

The language of the Beautiful is the "I" form or the first person singular. You can only learn this language through contemplation, self-reflection and looking back. By reflecting on your behaviour and on how you have handled things, you will discover your own hidden agendas and the qualities and talents that you have not drawn on.

A world of unlimited riches and opportunities will open to you, a world that is invisible for those who have only learnt how to observe the world through the "it" and the "we" lens. What is more, it opens a third way of observing. Alongside the "monological" way of looking through the "it" lens and the "dialogical" way of looking through the "we" lens, a "translogical" way of observing will develop, a way that you can only gain access to via the "I" lens. By "translogical" we mean a way of thinking that transcends logical and mental thought. As a source of information, intuition is just as valuable as objective facts and figures, except if you only believe in the "it" world (and as we see it, such a way of looking at things has no credibility).

DIFFERENTIATE OR SEPARATE   5

There is no denying the fact that making a distinction between "it", "we" and "I" ways of thinking has played a major role in the development of our society. Wilber refers to it in terms of the "dignity of modernity". Making a distinction between "we" and "it" has freed us from domination by the church's view of the universe and how it is formed, and so we can now see objectively (the "it" perspective) that the earth is round and not the centre of the universe as the church ("we") claimed for such a long time. Making such a distinction has enabled science to go its own way without having to conform to fundamentalist belief system dogma. Making a distinction between "I" and "we" has meant that the individual ("I") has been able to acquire individual rights that the church and the state ("we") can no longer ignore, as evidenced (and very well) in the Declaration of Human Rights.

Making a distinction between "I" and "it" means that the individual in general ("I") can no longer conclude that an apprehended object ("it") is real because he or she believes it is real. Making such a distinction has enabled quackery to be seen for what it is and medical science to develop: just two instances out of the many blessings conferred.

The world of management forms no exception to the rule. Initially, literature pertaining to management placed a somewhat one-sided emphasis on "it"-based thinking. Greater interest in "we"-based thinking has developed over time, with the effect that more attention has been paid to corporate culture, there has been greater emphasis on cooperation and encouragement of teamwork, and there has been a switch to seeking the common good and a striving for collectivity. During the past ten years, there has also been a growing interest in the "I" perspective, as witnessed by the greater emphasis on personal development plans, our feelings, the things we are passionate about, individual commitment and suchlike.

No problems so far. The ability to differentiate is a useful attribute. To make it bear fruit, though, it needs to be integrated: we have to learn to look at the world through three sets of eyes simultaneously and, with the enhanced awareness that this brings, look back on the situation in question. This is not what seems to be happening at the current point in time, however. Rather, what we seem to be doing is differentiating, then separating and returning to what we have always done, namely thinking from a one-dimensional point of view instead of a three-dimensional one.

As we hope you have been able to see from what we have already said, each way of looking at the world provides a perspective all of its own: different points of departure will be chosen and different viewpoints considered, different issues will be seen as important and there will be different priorities.

The "it" side tries to be involved in matters that are objectively present and as such real (Real and True), the "we" side is concerned with the Good, and the "I" side is concerned with matters whose outcome is personal fulfilment (Beauty or Splendour).

Things can go wrong, however, because we have a tendency to believe that some problems can be resolved by taking the "it" approach, some by taking the "we" approach and some by taking the "I" approach. As we have come to see things, this is wrong: every problem requires a unified approach. We are too inclined to think that if there is a particular way into a problem, there must be a solution along that line. We jump to the conclusion that if the problem can be identified as an "it" type of problem, the solution must also have the nature of an "it" solution. It is not so: there is not a single problem that can only be resolved via (for example) an objective analysis and approach.

This is quite an audacious statement. If our conclusion is correct, the consequences are mind-boggling.

Striving simultaneously for Beauty, Truth and the Good is a complex matter, because you are trying to see the situation from all three angles simultaneously. What makes this so difficult is that you run the threat of losing sight of other matters, or worse still, of disqualifying them and dismissing them as irrelevant.

Take, for example, ISO certification courses. Such courses are virtually always typical "it" affairs in which an attempt is made to describe processes as completely, as objectively and as closely to reality as possible: no easy task. The assumption is that describing processes will lead to greater predictability and controllability, and hence greater manageability, and that the eventual outcome will be a higher level of quality. In short, the greater the objectivity the better the quality. As an approach, this lacks all credibility: it is just not true. If the approach takes no account of corporate culture matters and individual involvement, instead seeing them as side issues, the ISO certification will in all probability result in frustration rather than in quality.

Things are going wrong if differentiation along the lines of "it", "we" and "I" leads to division or dissociation. This is precisely what is happening on a large scale. To be able to understand this disastrous development, you have to realize that they are not just different views: they are realities or hypothetical worlds, each with its own language and its own approach. And until we become trilingual people, "it"-style thinkers will continue to try and resolve "we" and "I" problems by means of "it"-style thinking. It simply will not work.

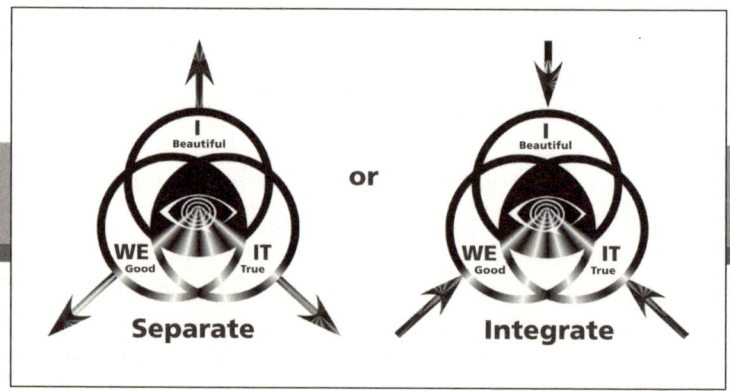

The issue is learning how to become a trilingual person by taking an interest in the language of the other worlds. The keyword is, in fact, *interest*.

It is precisely a lack of interest that can turn a scientific perspective ("it" ways of thinking) from a blessing into a curse. Whenever the scientific perspective loses its interest in subjectivity and individuality, the result will be a narrowing of consciousness. With our rational minds, restricting and narrowing our consciousness will end up becoming a fear of losing control. The only way out might well seem the path of violence. So we use force to try and get the "we" and the "I" under control: banning, denying, fighting or devouring the uncontrollable. An "it"-style coup will have the effect of turning the world into a dry, poverty-stricken, uninspired, lifeless wasteland where relationships have no place. A wasteland organization is one in which personal development is reduced to a check-off system, in which every employee has to hand in a personal development plan and cultural development is reduced to pretty posters on the wall showing the "cultural keys". Self-knowledge is reduced to a list of multiple-choice answers which tell you what Enneagram type you belong to, what your learning style is, what team role suits you most and what your personal qualities are. In short, who you are and how you have to go about self-improvement. Your PDP (Personal Development Plan) will be just one of many, and instead of delving into your own world of experiences you will have turned yourself into a project, complete with stages, supervision instruments and documents requiring decisions.

Do not be tempted to think that things are much better on the "I" side of things. From that perspective, we are inclined to think that as long as our creativity and inspiration is flowing, we are heading in the right direction. The outside world is cold, unfeeling and inhuman, and often not beautiful. We are less interested in objectivity, structure and common ground, preferring personal growth, freedom and awareness. And this is precisely its weakness: lack of interest in collective matters and objective reality can turn an individual perspective from a blessing into a curse. Instead of seeing that without structure, freedom is an illusion, structure is disposed of because it is regarded as limiting individual freedom.

Whenever the individual loses interest in objective reality and in things that are social, the result will be a narrowing of consciousness which takes the form of a fear of becoming absorbed into the great anonymous mass or of being offered up like a pawn in a system whose rules cannot be fathomed. Hardly any wonder that the individual will fight to the bitter end rather than risk such a fate.

If we adopt the "we" way of thinking we will want to enhance the company's corporate culture, encourage cooperation and promote value-based work practices. What will interest us is how we deal with each other and how we interact. Seen through "we" eyes, individuality is of secondary importance. The individual has to take the back seat and has a duty to adapt to the collective norm of Goodness. Conform or you are out. Objective reality may also be offered up without much reservation if a good feeling is at stake.

It is precisely this lack of interest in individuality and objectivity that can turn a social perspective from a blessing into a curse. Whenever there is a loss of social interest in individuality and objectivity, the result will also be a narrowing of consciousness which takes the form of a fear of losing communality and falling apart. The "we" type of thinking, then, becomes a constricting straightjacket of prescriptive rules with no room for personal development.

To generalize, *interest* is more inclined to promote integration and *indifference* dissociation. However, if our conclusions are correct, interest as we have described it above is likely to achieve more effective results than indifference.

Sounds logical, doesn't it?

Then why don't we see more of it?

In our everyday lives, problems will always manifest themselves initially as "it", "we" or "I" problems. The following three tips may help you broaden your approach and thus make it a more integrated one. We have found that they work for us.

1 If the problem manifests itself as an "it" problem, focus on *sustainability*.

2 If the problem manifests itself as a "we" problem, focus on *inclusiveness*.

3 If the problem manifests itself as an "I" problem, focus on *individual responsibility*.

They work because all three – sustainability, inclusiveness and individual responsibility – have the effect of expanding the focus of attention, thereby expanding our consciousness. A focus on sustainability will expand the time frame that is applicable, a focus on inclusiveness will increase the numbers of those involved, and a focus on taking personal responsibility will expand the field of co-responsibility since you will come to see yourself as a co-creator and not as a victim.

With an "it" problem, there is a tendency to look at the facts and figures only and to focus on measurable short-term results. If the problem cannot be measured there is no way of dealing with it, and so it will be dropped. Facts and figures have an aura of being the absolute truth. We forget all too quickly that the truths that they represent are only apparent truths, or at the very most only half truths. We really do start to believe in them. They draw your attention away from anything of a subjective nature or having to do with interaction. Facts and figures, then, start to dictate what goes on. They narrow our field of consciousness, possess us and extinguish our interest in the "we" and "I" sides of the matter. An "it"-based approach gradually swallows you up, as it were, making it impossible for you to see there is a reality other than the reality that is presented to you as objective reality. Putting the focus of attention on *sustainability* helps to reverse this process. By including long-term and ecological effects as well as the short-term ones in your evaluation, you will expand your field of awareness, and the things that cannot be as easily measured will attract your attention. This is only logical because since you are focusing on both the now and the future (and the future cannot be objectively measured, nor can sustainability be objectively proven) you will have to develop an interest in your own propositions, in things of a subjective nature and in your sensitivity to things. You will no longer be able to dismiss them as irrelevant, and you will thereby open the door to "we" and "I" perspectives on the matter.

With a "we" problem, there will be a tendency to make the situation a "we" versus "them" one and to focus solely on the interests of those whom you call "us": those that you yourself have delineated. In other words, there will be a search for solutions of an exclusive rather than inclusive kind. If you are thinking in inclusive terms, you will be constantly expanding the circle of people involved. You will not exclude anybody and this will cause an expansion of your awareness. A necessary precondition for this is *interest*. If you really are interested in the other you will hear more, see more and feel more.

With an "I" problem there will be a tendency to seek the solution outside yourself, within the other. It is always easy to blame an undesirable situation on somebody else. The same applies to organizational frustrations. There, too, it is easy to shift the blame onto the system, or onto a lack of clarity in the structure, or onto a lack of vision in those in charge. "If only they...", then everything would improve. By changing the focus of attention to your own responsibility and investigating your own part in the situation that has developed, you will expand your awareness and thereby automatically make your focus more *inclusive*, simply because you are including and involving yourself instead of the opposite. By taking responsibility for yourself, you will also start to look for more *sustainable* solutions, because it will become very clear that your initiative is also required. And why would you take the initiative if it did not result in a sustainable solution? After all, it is only in your own best interests.

Another interesting way of learning to observe through three lenses simultaneously is by asking yourself what types of information are available and how you can acquire that information.

1 "It"-style information can be obtained from data derived from measurements.
2 "We"-style information can be obtained by listening to others' stories.
3 "I"-style information can be obtained by opening yourself up to impressions and sensing things.

Hard facts are the sort of information that your "it" side can operate with. They often turn out to be less hard than they seemed, but with a certain amount of alertness you can distinguish hard facts from foggy assumptions. A precondition for this is not assuming that statistics are, by definition, facts.

Stories and rumours are always doing the rounds. "Guess what the latest news is?", "Have you heard that…?" People like to talk about other people. What do they talk about (and more particularly, what don't they talk about)? It is rarely facts, more often opinions. The "we" side sees stories as being just as real as facts are to the "it" side. The stories all form a source of information about the "we" side: information that is available to all.

Impressions, premonitions, intuitions: all of these provide you with information from your own inner world, information that can give you valuable leads as long as you are no stranger to that world (the "I" world). But if you are, it can bring confusion rather than enlightenment. One of the advantages of greater self-knowledge is that you are more able to separate the wheat from the chaff where external information is concerned. As such, self-knowledge is certainly no luxury (as is often claimed), but an absolute prerequisite for anyone in a managerial position, because without self-knowledge not only will you be unfamiliar with the language of "I", you will also be lacking all the information that "I" can provide.

If you make use of all three ways of gathering information, there will be more sustainability and greater inclusiveness in what you do, and more taking of personal responsibility. Reliance on only one of the three sources will simplify things too much, and will restrict you, providing you with information that is probably only partly reliable, and consequently lacking in credibility.

It will probably have become clear by now that the three forms of reality that have been mentioned each require us to have certain capabilities or qualities. These will differ from one person to the next. What you choose to do will depend on who you are.

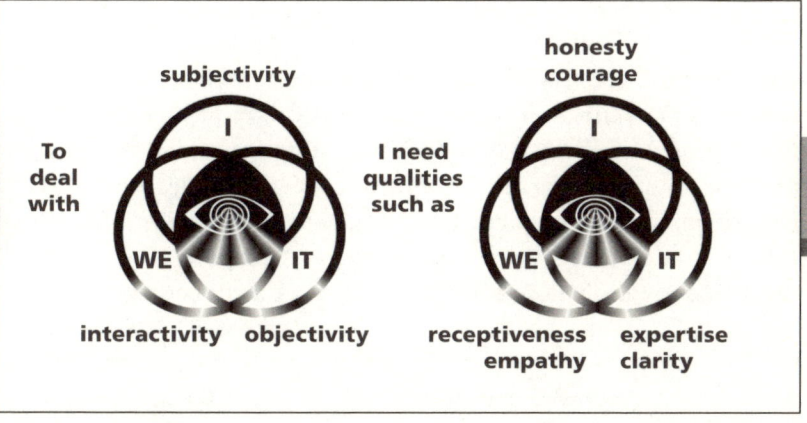

In my (Daniel's) case, my "it" side requires me to be interested in objective data and to test this data critically. This requires me to have qualities such as professionality and clarity. Since these are qualities that are part of me, I will have a good chance of success.

My "we" side requires me to have an interest in relational matters. What I need are qualities such as receptiveness and empathy. I am not by nature as well equipped in these qualities. This does not mean that I cannot be receptive or show empathy, just that they require more effort, and so I have to pay closer attention to them.

My "I" side requires me to show an interest in myself and in my inner world. To be able to adequately cope with my own subjective nature I need honesty and courage: the honesty to look critically at my own qualities, the pitfalls that may await me, my challenges and the things that get my back up (my "allergies"), and the courage to translate this into deeds and interaction. I have less difficulty with honesty and courage than with being prepared to make time for reflection.

Everybody really ought to do a self-assessment along these lines and use it to find an integrated way of dealing with issues.

As we see it, three-dimensional thinking, feeling and acting is what makes the difference between a manager and a leader. The ability to see through three sets of eyes simultaneously is what gives us depth, and this opens the door to a world that is full of new challenges and new opportunities. By paying ongoing attention to his or her commitment to what he or she is doing, to collective values and to effective systems, a leader can create an organization which is firing on all cylinders at all levels, which has a vigorous corporate culture in all departments, and whose work processes have a vital energy.

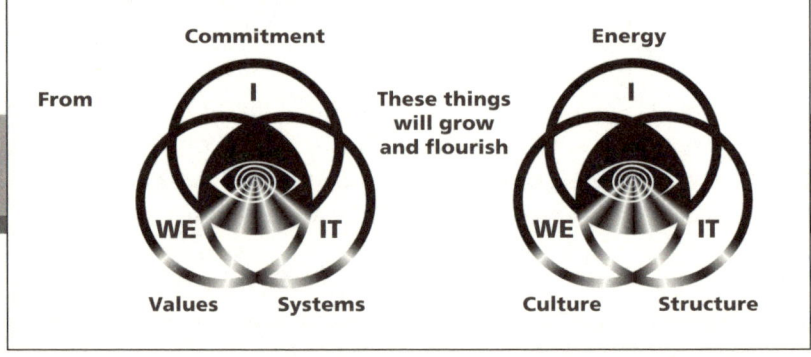

Have we achieved this at Philip Morris Holland? Only to a certain extent. It is by no means enough.

A lot more could be said about the new model, but let us not forget that it arose in retrospect, as we looked back on what we had done within Philip Morris Holland. A lot of things went well there, though not all.

What now follows are a number of accounts of actual experiences as seen through the eyes of Guust and with a "recap" appraisal of them by Daniel. We hope that the combination of account, experience and appraisal will do justice to the whole truth and that it will contribute to unlocking the nature of inspiration and unmasking one-sided truths for what they are.

PART II
FROM MODEL TO PRACTICE

7 SHOWING APPRECIATION

There we were: a management team not yet really at ease with each other. It was our first "rural retreat" since my appointment as General Director, and what I wanted to do was look into the values that we – the management team – wanted to uphold. Instead of doing a lot of talking, we were making a collage out of bits and pieces that appealed to us from magazines. There was a story behind each picture. The idea was that by acting out these stories and expanding on them we would get to the essence of the values that played an implicit role in our lives.

I saw these values as an extension of our team, as a sort of ideal image. This is how we wanted to deal with each other and how we wanted others within the organization to deal with each other. It was our statement of intention in relation to the corporate culture we envisioned.

At the end of the first session we had listed some five core values that we wanted to jointly uphold:

- Transparency,
- Respect,
- Integrity,
- Dedication,
- Inclusiveness.

The most logical course of action would now have been to draw up a plan of communication along structural lines (the "it" side) and then to present the core values we had settled on to the organization. Along with this we would explain what the core values stood for. Our definitions of transparency, respect, integrity, dedication and inclusiveness as well as an explanation of why it was important to operate on the basis of these values would be put into a glibly worded mission statement and then disseminated to everyone in an affirmative and appealing way via the intranet. Three months later and everybody would be familiar with the core values in this jazzed-up form. People would start enthusiastically applying the values in their day-to-day situations. The enthusiasm would be infectious, and the job finished before you could say go. Things would be kept on the boil by performing a check every now and then, just to make sure that everybody knew the five values off by heart. Alas, I knew all too well that this just would not work!

Instead of laying down the core values right from the start, I asked myself whether the rest of the organization would support them. Perhaps they were advocates of other values. Because of my uncertainty in this regard, I decided to invite a group of young people from various departments to undergo the same process and to note what they arrived at. The selection procedure was unusual in that for once we did not select the next-down management level but a youthful mix of people selected from a representative number of departments. I had good hopes that these young people would dare to stand up for their own opinions. The group was given the original name of "the Culture Club".

After cutting and pasting, talking and doing presentations (a program identical to that which we had followed six weeks previously) they arrived at four core values which bore a surprising resemblance to ours. As such, it was not difficult to adopt the values they formulated:

- Openness (as against Transparency),
- Respect,
- Integrity,
- Giving the best you can (as against Dedication).

Inclusiveness was not included. Inclusiveness is not really a core value, more a certain state of awareness. With inclusiveness, the issue is to involve as many other people in your core values as you can. The more people you involve in your core values, the more valid and pertinent the core values will be and the greater their "added value". For those who like formulas, you could state the following:

$$Values \times Inclusiveness = Added\ Value$$

To put it in other words, by excluding others you take away the *value* in values.
An arrangement was made for the Culture Club to initiate discussions on the core values in their own surroundings. Not only did we have our doubts about this, but the members of the Culture Club were also unsure about whether the approach would catch on. It was up to the management team to put our heads together and see how we could implement the core values. The issue here was, of course, how to connect the "I" and the "it" sides of things.

I went about establishing the "it" side connections by telling the rest of the organization that they could always call me to account where those values were concerned. In other words, if I did anything, made any decisions or came out with comments that clashed with those values, I would expect to be taken to task by the others. I had a personal involvement in those values and I did not mind who knew this. As far as this was concerned, I was accountable to everyone.

Without feedback, there can never be a change of corporate culture. Just as valuable as good feedback, is showing appreciation for deeds and behaviour that do match the cultural ideal. Just as compliments go hand-in-hand with joy and pleasure, the giving of negative feedback is unavoidably linked to pain and sorrow. Providing feedback that strengthens a person should be elevated to an art. There is no art to cutting somebody down.

The "it" core values, after we had integrated them into our management model, came to look like the following:

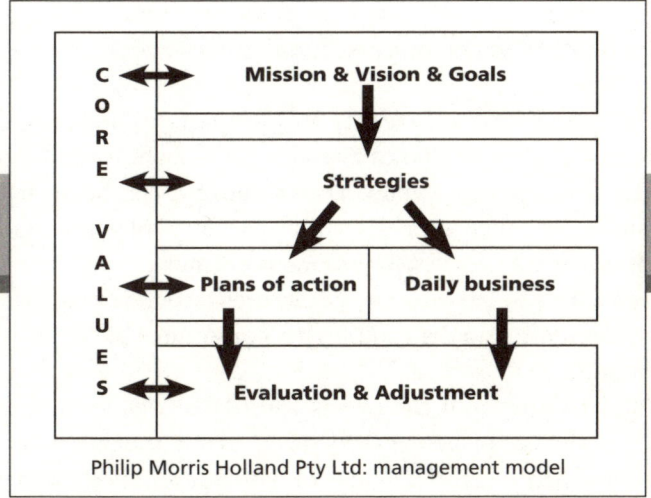

Philip Morris Holland Pty Ltd: management model

This model showed how the core values were tied to the system side of the business and to its operations. Our goals, plans, deeds and dealings were constantly checked against the core values, and if they clashed they were definitely not allowed. Where these values were concerned, we were not making any exceptions now or in the future. Consequently, all our dealings and decisions were checked for conformity to them. Though it was often automatically done, it was sometimes necessary to make this a conscious part of our agenda. Tying things in with each other in such a voluntary way is completely at odds with the enforced methods typical of many "it"-style organizations, where things have to be hammered in or else the core values will degenerate into nothing more than a glorified statement of intention.

■■■■■■ RECAP

What is it that makes this seemingly straightforward account so special? There is nothing new about formulating values, putting them down on paper and disseminating them. Few people would quarrel with the notion of values being important. The real issue is that each of the three types of reality look upon some values as having more worth (or in other words, more reality) than others.

1 The "it" perspective sees reality as a property of objective things. With facts and figures you can determine probability and work out what the chances are. Money has a value that can be determined. The stock exchange rate determines what a business is worth. Worth is more or less synonymous with monetary value. 2 Seen through the "we" perspective, values are the basis of culture and a value represents a way of gauging the correctness of behaviour and interaction.
3 The "I" lens filters out the things you like or dislike, and colours your experiences of people and things. How much worth something has depends on the extent to which it is experienced as real and genuine. Worth is derived from experience. To value a person is to give him his due.

Directing an organization that is driven by its values is more than just formulating and writing down a few nice terms that nobody could object to. It is to infuse life into what is real, what has worth and what is a value as seen through all three forms of reality. You could say that it is to learn to *value* value.

In many of the team sessions we availed ourselves of techniques other than the usual management techniques. They included improvisation, martial arts, aikido, song and dance, and a lot of other forms of artistic expression. They had a dual purpose. In the first place, such techniques bring us into contact with other sides of ourselves and other sources of inspiration – sources we are not used to paying much attention to. The information that derives from those aspects of ourselves and those sources is immensely valuable. You could talk about values until you are blue in the face; applying our visual capacities to give form to our vision – using our imaginative powers – is usually quicker. As well as this, the principles that infuse such methods often provide useful analogies for day-to-day situations, showing us how we can deal more effectively with others as well as ourselves. To take aikido as an example, it has four principles as its basis: inviting participation, moving along with the others, giving direction and letting go. These were precisely the things that Guust did.

1 **Inviting participation**
   Instead of doing it all himself, Guust started out by inviting participation. His team members were invited to tell their own stories about the things that they were passionate about. He then invited a group of young people to join him in the thought process. The next move was to invite the organization as a whole to call him to account personally and to confront him with any breach of the core values. His opening move was consistently that of inviting participation.
2 **Moving along with the others**
   When people responded to his invitation, Guust made sure that he moved along with those who had accepted it. Moving along with others is the opposite of clashing with them. To do this is to enter into an initial dialogue with the other with the goal of finding out

what it is that the other wishes to say and what he or she really means. What you yourself think is not the main thing: if you give your own opinion you could quickly find yourself clashing with the other, with monologue, polarization, conflict and use of force as the end results. What you need to do is get to know the other: to meet people face-to-face and to establish understanding. This approach made it possible for Guust to easily correlate the five core values that his team had formulated with the values that the Culture Club had put together.

3 **Giving direction**

If you only go along with the others and never add anything of any value of your own, your "added value" will lose its entire worth. That is why it is important to give some direction by saying what you yourself see, think, feel, believe and desire. If you do this in a non-confrontational manner, you may be astonished at the ready reception you will receive. One way of giving direction is by giving feedback, but feedback of the type that empowers the other. You can also give direction by being consistent in the way that you integrate the values into the management model and by checking on a daily basis whether the decisions that have been made are consistent with the core values that have been formulated.

4 **Letting go**

Finally, it is always important to let go. By letting go we mean not spending the whole day forcing things, convincing others or controlling things, but having faith in the process. The members of the Culture Club were left entirely free to discuss the core values with their colleagues in the way that they chose. Trust was needed here, not a plan. By letting go you give the other the space to find his or her own way of doing things. It does not, of course, mean dropping everything and dismissing them from your attention. By keeping things within your field of attention, issuing the next invitation will come naturally, thereby initiating the next cycle of inviting participation, joining in, giving direction and letting go.

"How did it go?" the managerial secretary asked. "Oh, fine. There were at least 20 people at the meeting. I had the impression that my talk went down well: at least, they listened very attentively," answered the Director. Making contact with the shop floor, knowing what concerns people have: every director or manager will agree that this is very important. What you often encounter are organized meetings, in which the director gives a talk and staff are invited to ask questions. A good thing, this sort of session, with or without breakfast or coffee.

"How did it go?" Leo asks Fred, a machine operator and Leo's co-worker.

"Oh, pretty much like last time. The same impersonal talk and any questions that were put he didn't understand."

"So why did you go?"

"Because my supervisor had already told me three times that it was my turn, and that if I didn't go, nobody else would."

"He who has ears to hear but doesn't use them won't hear anything either."

"What did you say?"

"Just talking about deafness."

"Whose deafness?"

"Ours."

"You're saying I'm deaf?"

"Not just you. It."

"Well, who'd believe anything around here!"

It is hard to establish contact with the shop floor, and for various reasons. There may be obstacles of various kinds: lack of time, for example, or the size of the organization. It may be the perception that, anyway, the staff would not say what they were thinking: after all, who would be interested when it is facts that count?

Establishing contact with the shop floor is important. If you are pre-pared to listen and take in what is being said, you will hear a lot of things. If you combine what you hear with facts and figures as well as with the things that you feel intuitively, the result will be infor-mation you can use. This is precisely how I managed to obtain the information I needed in relation to the broad issues we had to give our attention to.

It all started with *gemba*, the Japanese word for the shop floor, or so I was told during a *kaizen* workshop. It is a straightforward notion: go to the shop floor and listen to the concerns that are voiced there. Then adopt the improvements suggested there immediately. As soon as I heard this I decided to introduce *gemba*. We gave the term a personal twist: for us it stood for *Guust and his Mates like Being Around*. Once a week, two members of the management team paid a visit to one of the company's departments. The department determined what was on the agenda. It might be a presentation, a question-answering session or a practical problem. In view of the size of the organization (1,850 employees), planning it all properly was quite a daunting task. It en-ded up taking us a year to cover all the departments. The quantity of information, first-hand experiences and impressions that we, the ma-nagerial team, got out of these sessions was enormous. I was sincere in wanting to do something with the concerns within the departments. It was, of course, not possible to resolve every problem and there were some matters that just could not be resolved in a few simple steps or even resolved at all. As long as the employees were being taken seri-ously, this really did not bother anybody. What I did notice was that a number of my colleagues had difficulty with these *gembas*. They had difficulty meeting people face-to-face and they found it hard to show their own vulnerability. Although a director obviously cannot possibly know everything, admitting as much is not only a terrifying prospect for him or her, it is virtually a mortal sin within the broader Philip Morris corporate culture.

Anyone who has a managerial position finds it hard to show their own vulnerability. However, there is no reason for it to be difficult. All you usually have to do is show that you care. Employees will not ask the impossible. Just listen and give an honest answer to the questions you are asked. Anyone in a managerial position who does this will be amply rewarded with respect and trust.

A year of *gemba* was enough for me to conclude that it had a lot going for it. As an approach, it enabled me to identify certain cultural issues more clearly and to define even more closely the broader issues that needed to be addressed. An essential precondition was the connecting up of first-hand experiences with the facts and figures and my intuition. In my perception, the only down-side was that I did not get enough information: the *gemba* visits were just not frequent enough.

It was this that prompted me to start *Guust online*. Once again, there was a simple idea behind it: I would write a monthly column for the intranet and invite the employees to react to whatever contention I made or opinion I put forward. A dozen or so people would then be invited to exchange views with me on the subject over breakfast. Not only could I transmit messages to the entire organization, but it would also give me the opportunity to receive unfiltered signals emanating from the organization. Alongside this, I spent as much time as I could walking around. I made sure that there was a space of half an hour between meetings so that I could take full advantage of any unexpected encounter. During the course of time, coffee breaks (ten minutes in my office while we had a tea or coffee) became increasingly frequent. It is my firm conviction that you can never put too much time into face-to-face contacts.

As a rule, organizations spend too much time collecting facts and figures and too little time in collecting impressions and others' experiences. A better time division (given that you put 30% of your time into gathering information) would be:

10% others' experiences,
10% feelings/impressions,
10% facts and figures.

During the Middle Ages, the king got his tales from his fool, the court jester. Nowadays, the only fool is the king who fails to listen.

■■■■■ RECAP

You could be excused for wondering what was so special about *gembas* and *Guust online*. Skeptics will immediately say that being open to other people is only natural. However, the point is not that there is anything special about it, but that these are examples of ways in which you can manage in an organic way. It is not that you are talking to people because they like this so much or to motivate your co-workers, but because you care about people. It is also the only way of digging up the information you need to make balanced decisions. Managers who try to motivate or inspire their staff are failing to see that motivation and inspiration do not derive from external sources and are not a goal in themselves, but are a logical consequence of managing in an organic way. To think that you can provide motivation for people is arrogant and symptomatic of the "it" style of thinking: thinking that everything can be manipulated and can be planned. *Motivation is a consequence and must not be a goal in itself.* You can rely on the fact that people are quite capable of providing their own motivation. As the manager, your job is to provide direction of an organic nature. Do this, and motivation, inspiration, passion, dynamism, vitality and so on will follow automatically.

Our "it" side tends to want to look at the facts and figures only, and after analyzing them, to come into action: pushing, directing, controlling and exercising power. If you fail to link them up with your impressions, ideas and what the personal experiences of others within the organization are telling you, you will fail to achieve lasting results. It is by no means unusual for a planned course of action to be either forcibly pursued or to die a slow death from lack of inspiration and broad support.

Our "we" side inclines us to only listen to others' experiences and to rumours. Without objective data and subjective impressions, the most you will be able to obtain is short-term profit.

Our "I" side inclines us to act according to how we sense things. If it feels good, then do it; if not, then leave it alone. But intuitive feelings that are not put to a reality test can be misleading, particularly when you are unaware why it is that you are feeling that way. *Gembas* and *Guus online* demonstrate nicely how you can go about managing organically by listening to yourself and to what others have to say.

9 SAYING "YES"

"We really ought to reduce absenteeism a bit more," said the Director. "For a company operating three shifts, 5% off sick is a bit on the high side. Could you analyze the present absentee rate and come up with some suggestions for improvement? If we worked more on prevention and supervision we should be able to get better short-term results. I'd like to see a plan of action in two weeks' time."

Sounds familiar? Management teams hear this sort of thing all too often in meetings. The absenteeism rate cannot possibly be improved in any lasting way by analyzing the figures and drawing up a plan of action. Such a short-sighted approach may well produce a brief flurry of short-term results, but any lasting changes require a more holistic and organic approach.

"Would you like to sponsor my group?"
"What group?" I asked.
"A group of employees that have come down sick and so they have to do a retraining course."

I vividly remember Frank asking me this. My immediate response was "yes", though I had no idea what I was letting myself in for. For me, development begins with saying "yes", with showing you care, with being open to the things that come your way. Opportunities are always there in abundance. This was just one of them. The problem is that we do not always see them as being opportunities, rather as an imposition, as even more work (and aren't we busy enough already?).

It was an invitation to participate that had a good feel to it and which aroused my interest without my knowing exactly what was expected of me. The group in question prompted an integration policy that has had impressive results.

What came to be christened "Guust's group" was a group of people who were temporarily on non-active, because they were suffering from various illnesses and could no longer carry out their former jobs. Learning a new trade would be a real challenge for all of them. Frank, a gentle Human Relations employee with a heart of gold, had come up with the idea of the group. Letting these people pursue a joint training course at their current workplace would help them pick up the knack of retraining. They would then follow a retraining course and be given another job within the company. There was certainly nothing wrong with the idea, but it had not been fleshed out at all and ran the risk of becoming just another feel-good group with noble intentions. Active reintegration required more: it required involvement; a cozy "we" feeling was not enough on its own.

The personal stories and the fears of the people who formed the group had an impact on me, and I decided to re-examine the company's reintegration policy. A "body shop" approach is the best way of describing the policy up to that point. You got sick and went on non-active. After a period of time the matter of reintegration came up. There was a policy of putting as many employees as possible back into their old workplaces. If this did not work, the "body shop" was the next step. A philosophic older gentleman by the name of Adrie took you under his wing. Adrie went the rounds of various managers within the company and asked them if there was any chance of finding a bit of a spot for the employee in question. Nobody was very keen on having employees of this sort, because not only did they need your attention and thus took up your time, but if they were a success, you as manager ran the risk of having to create a permanent position for the employee. He or she was, after all, in your department. In all his years there and despite the best of intentions, this was the fate of a lot of the employees that came Adrie's way. It was unavoidable that the employees in question felt unwelcome in their new work surroundings right from the very start. Fear of no longer having a permanent job would put these people under psychological pressure, again resulting in illness. They could ill afford this, because it only confirmed the stigma of being a weakling. An unfortunate and negative spiral of events would result.

It was because of this that I decided to take stock of the facts. A project was the result. After an intensive stock-taking we were able to chart the number of employees we were sure would have to be placed on non-active because of the nature of their illnesses, which were often chronic ones. Their own accounts made it clear to us that on no account should those who were up for retraining be fobbed off with phony jobs. These people wanted to be given their full value and to be given real work. As a result of a new business system and simultaneously with starting the project, the company was faced with the necessity of having to reclassify its entire spare parts system. It was a gigantic administrative job. Instead of calling in temps to do the job, we decided to offer the job to those whose illnesses were such that we expected to have to put them on non-active in the immediate future. Simultaneously with this real work, we would offer them a retraining course. A prerequisite was that everyone be prepared to consider his or her own situation and on the basis of a two-day workshop make their own choices. The group was assigned a manager of its own (Erwin) as well as a contact person within the Human Resources department (Babs). They were also given a room of their own, so that they could provide each other with mutual support. Nine months later (the expected duration of the project), we would try to give everyone another permanent job within the company. However, no guarantees were given.

After individual discussions, eleven employees took up the invitation. The project got under way. After five months of working, workshops, career guidance and, most particularly, personal attention and cooperation, Babs and Erwin came up with their reports. Before the pilot scheme, absenteeism was at 25%; five months later it was 0%! The reclassification project was well on track and was scoring very good results. The participants were starting to get an idea of what they wanted to do in the future. There was one problem, however: internally, not a single vacancy had arisen that could be filled by any one of these people. The project was due to finish in four months' time and the employees could not return to their old spots. What if there were no opportunities whatsoever for them? Without even so much as a pause for thought, I replied: "Don't worry about it; it will resolve itself."

What I did not want Babs and Erwin to know was that I did not know myself. I did, however, have a strong conviction that things would turn out all right. I would keep my eyes and ears open: the only thing I could do was to be alert.

Having faith that things will turn out all right does not mean that, having initiated something positive, all you have to do is rely on cosmic forces to do the rest. That is not the way things happen. Having faith in something means staying aware and alert, keeping your ears cocked, looking all around you and taking things in, running your mind over things and investigating any possibilities. If possibilities do arise, you should play in on them, but always in an appropriate way, not exerting any pressure or using any force.

The first opportunities came our way during the budget rounds. Because of the extra work, someone was looking for an additional administrative worker for his department. I asked him to go and have a chat with Babs: the pilot group probably had something to offer. That got the ball rolling. On this occasion too, I realized that invitation worked better than pressing on regardless, or forcing a decision. The new department had an equal right to make a genuine decision. We eventually managed to place ten of the eleven people in new jobs. This was a process whereby the participants and the departments were offered the opportunity to make responsible choices. It worked for ten of the eleven. It was very encouraging for those in a similar position.

We did have to say goodbye to one of the participants. He simply did not want to take the initiative. There comes a moment when you can do nothing more. This, too, is something that the organization has to accept.

The things we learned from this project were translated later into a copy-book integration policy. When the Gatekeeper Act (*Wet Poortwachter*) was formulated, it became clear that we were well in advance of our times.

Having a good policy and being well-intentioned are no assurance that people will learn how to take responsibility for themselves. This applies both to participants in courses like this one and to managerial staff. Individual responsibility is one of the things that you as a company cannot take over. An integration policy that looks great on paper is not enough. What it depends on is people like Erwin (the manager) and Babs dedicating themselves sincerely, unselfishly and with a passion and an awareness of the values at stake to such people, but without taking their problems on board. However touching someone's story is, that person has to take responsibility for him or herself.

In the hands of Human Resources staff who are lacking in awareness, the same integration policy can easily give rise to human dramas. I want to stress again that for a policy as has been described above to work, ongoing communication is essential. The moment it starts to be applied clinically as a Human Resources tool, it will turn into yet another soulless "it" procedure. It will have lost its credibility.

■■■■■■ **RECAP**

A leader with a dominating "it" mentality will simply analyze the issue in terms of the facts and will draw up a plan of action. Something in Guust made him take up Frank's invitation. He then took his responsibility as a manager to implement a different kind of policy.

Frank let himself be guided by his socially minded "we" feeling: he communicated a request to management to contribute to his initiative. What he ended up getting was, however, much more than he asked for. He received commitment ("I") and structure ("it"), and with them a lasting solution. Taken together, long- and short-term sick leave within the organization as a whole dropped by 20% from 5% to 4% and, instead of anxiety, sick employees regained their hopes of being able to start again.

An essential part of Guust's approach was a focus on individual responsibility, sustainability and inclusiveness. It left no room for those who did not want to take responsibility for themselves or who thought in terms of exclusivity, and it categorically rejected cosmetic solutions: solutions which may have had short-term appeal but which would end up a disaster in the long term. It meant that there had to be clear boundaries to what was and what was not tolerated. The company was now much more receptive to personal initiative and to finding creative solutions, and less receptive to those who did not want more freedom or to take more responsibility. More so than previously, this meant taking leave of various people. Organic leadership demands clear boundaries and consistency in dealing with things.

To start by saying "yes" does not mean to continue that way. Starting with a "yes" is much the same as the aikido principle of moving along. A "yes" initiates dialogue; a "no" usually monologue. When we do workshops, we practice doing this not only via aikido: improvisational theater also operates from the same principles. If you start out by saying "no", this puts an end to the improvised performance: it short-circuits all dialogue. Things come to a standstill because no connections have been established. Saying "yes" is saying that you want to be involved. You have to wait for connection and trust to be established before you start to play, to experiment, to put out feelers and to see what happens if you say "no". It is only then that you can start to give some direction and, in turn, to let go.

Improvisational theater is based on the notion that if you take a certain *attitude* you will provoke a certain *interaction*. This is, of course, not restricted to theater of this type: it is just as applicable to the theater of our daily lives. Your own attitude sets off a certain pattern of interaction. This is why it is so important for everyone in a managerial position to be aware of how he or she comes across, what his or her motives, urges, conscious and unconscious attitudes and personal quirks are. Do your character quirks come over as pleasantness or as lack of good grace?

If you start out by saying "no", not only will this call a halt to any dialogue ("we"), but the channel to your intuition ("I") will jam up and you will not be able to access the information that is awaiting you: information of the type that transcends logic. There was no logic behind Guust's initial reaction of "yes": it was an intuitive response, which he then followed up without losing sight of the facts and figures. To start out by saying "yes" is particularly difficult for people who mainly put their trust in their "it" side, since that part of oneself only wants to say "yes" to the things that are objectively true and thus can be trusted, brought under control and checked. Your "it" side does not permit a "yes" to things that cannot be proven. You will be more inclined to assume that they are not true until there is irrefutable proof to the contrary. If this is the only way in which your reality operates, you will certainly hesitate before you say "yes". You won't rush in with your eyes only half open! But if you do not look out, your very circumspection will make you blind to two other forms of reality that are highly relevant.

By saying "yes" you will connect up with what you really want. If you are confronted with something that you really do not want, it is much easier to say "no" if you know what it is you would prefer to say "yes" to. In other words, if that "no" of yours derives from a "yes" to something else, it will be much easier to hear if you also let your "yes" be heard. Start out by saying "yes" but keep on saying "yes" within yourself and maintain the connection with your inner vision, with what you really do want. To do this is to maintain your creativity, even if you do draw boundaries and say no.

10 TRUST

The "uptime project" was about reducing the time that the machinery was idle. The more hours a machine operates the better. Increasing the uptime was one of the company's main strategic goals. There are various ways of defining uptime, though this is not relevant to what follows. The figures mentioned do, however, have a factual basis.

The idea behind the uptime project was relatively simple: by increasing the factory's output we would stand a better chance of competing successfully with low-wage countries. Imagine it as follows: increasing factory turnover by 10%, for example, would produce approximately 10 billion extra production units. These 10 billion units would not require any additional investment, nor would any additional personnel have to be employed, since the existing staff would simply produce the additional volume. In fact, this additional 10 billion would neither cost any more in wage costs nor would there be any additional depreciation costs. Not a single low-wage country could compete with this. It was, of course, crucial that the employees be behind this strategy.

The first step was to get in touch with as many people as possible and explain the strategy to them, with the purpose of inviting as many people as possible to contribute to the plan. I spent a lot of time during the first year explaining the strategy. Those in managerial positions started to develop an interest in it too. During the Business Management course there were even two groups of supervisors who had chosen to do a case study of the matter for their final assignment. A jury of so-called experts would pass judgment on the completed case study and a presentation on it, and give it a mark. I was invited to witness the process.

High Speed versus Mid Speed

There were two presentations, one by the so-called High Speed group and the other by the Mid Speed group. To sum it up, the High Speed presentation revolved around the observation that there would be a much better uptime rate if the shift switchovers were better organized. The team used diagrams and analyses to demonstrate that there was considerable loss during the shift switchover and a reduction of this loss would mean a considerable increase in output. The plan was to get a task force to develop a new procedure for the shift changeover and put it into action. The machine operators were either not consulted or only minimally (I had a strong feeling that the group actually viewed the machine operators as the cause of the too low uptime). Management would then take things in hand and implement a new procedure. Better results were assured, and they would follow almost immediately.

The Mid Speed presentation was completely different. It too came up with analyses that showed that the uptime proposal could produce significant improvements, but just as I had always proposed, by looking for clever solutions rather than by working harder. This group's proposed approach was to discuss the uptime proposal with the machine operators and then jointly look for and implement ways of improving results. This group also finished its presentation by showing what improvements could be expected: in their view a 10% increase over a four year period could be achieved – a claim at any rate less spectacular than the High Speed claim.

Personally, I was very enthusiastic about the Mid Speed account. What the group was in fact saying was this:

- Uptime has a lot of potential for improvement.
- We do not know where to begin.
- There is no doubt in our minds that we must work jointly with the employees.
- We intend to bring them into it.
- We are fully confident that this will produce results.

Despite their slick presentation, the High Speed group did not give me the impression of having any real sense of involvement with the uptime project, and they made it very apparent that they did not intend to involve the employees. The expert jury awarded the group a pass with distinction. The Mid Speed group slunk off in disappointment and with a significantly lower mark. I disagreed completely with the expert jury, but had to content myself with taking the Mid Speed group aside and telling them that I was moved by their presentation and, like them, felt that theirs was the right approach.

Fortunately, they stuck to their approach. They achieved the 10% improvement earlier than they had expected. It was, however, touch and go: at a particular point in time they were on the point of losing faith. They invited me to come along and listen to their doubts and uncertainties. What they voiced to me was, "It won't work; we don't agree with each other; we're not making any progress; working out what to do is costing us too much of a struggle; our people are doubtful; we have to make choices but we just can't agree on them." These problems were put before me and I was asked for advice on how to proceed – as if I knew what the solution was.

There was one thing I did know, however: they had not stopped being involved with uptime. I told them that this phase was part of the process and that they were on the right track. They would get answers as long as they maintained good contact with each other.

I did not hear anything for a long time after that, though I did see the figures rise. A year later I brought it to their attention that they had already achieved their original goal, and complimented them on doing so. Their response astonished me: "This is only the start!" I will not easily forget the smiles on their faces.

And High Speed? Their analytical approach and logical plan ran aground, not producing a single improvement. In an open climate of mutual cooperation and personal commitment, there was no support for their one-sided "it"-style approach, and we eventually decided to appoint a different manager to do the difficult task of winning back trust. Trust is slow to gain and quick to lose!

▰▰▰ RECAP

The striking thing about the Uptime story was the lack of pressure, of *having* to do things, of jostling. Instead, there was a trust that it would all work out right if the right things were done.

But where on earth do you find the confidence that things will work out when the going is tough? What can you rely on then?

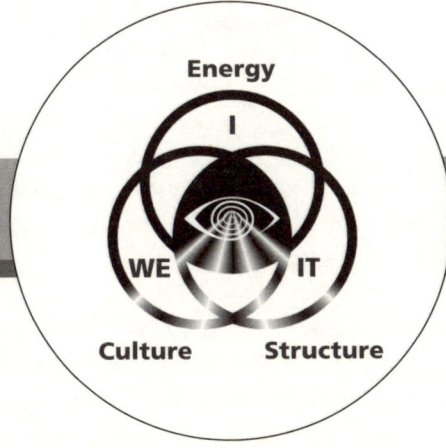

Guust's term "involvement" indicates where he derives his confidence from. If people feel involved with what they are doing, an essential prerequisite for success will have been met. On its own, though, it is not enough. In the long term, the only way to achieve lasting results is via individual zeal or commitment in combination with a corporate openness and willingness to work together on a structured approach.

Formulated in a different way, it could be said that what managers need to learn is to reflect, to analyze and to improvise. To reflect is to ponder how much you yourself feel involved and what your own motives are. Is this what I want, can I take it on, is it the right time to do it? Can I commit myself fully to it?

To analyze is to investigate what it is all about. What are the facts? What can these facts tell us? What are the causes and so on? What hints can they give us for finding solutions?

To improvise is to expand your capacity for deviating from the usual, for trying out different things, for being creative, for doing the exact opposite of the most obvious thing to do. Taken together, they make you a creative person and the team a creative team, and provide the energy to persevere when things do not look like working out. Taken together, they provide the fuel to continue. If one of these factors is missing, you will run aground; it will exhaust you. Aikido has an appropriate slogan for it: *outside one there is none*, which for me means that if you have not developed a single perspective from the three focal points and keep on seeing three separate worlds, you will only be seeing worthless illusions that do not have any credibility to them.

11   NOT DOING

During a January management meeting, I made the comment that within the organization was a desire not to succeed. I could not quite put my finger on it, but for several weeks, I had had the feeling that it was failure that the organization was striving for rather than success. The other members of the management team could not relate to the feeling at all and so I abandoned my vague notion. I later realized that this was one of the first occasions that I had come into clear contact with the organization's collective subconsciousness.

Relatively soon after the management meeting, we started negotiating a new collective labour agreement. Negotiating a collective labour agreement is an extraordinary process. You suddenly find yourself dealing with trade unions who claim to be championing the employees' interests: as though you yourself have never done this or have decided that other people's welfare is of absolutely no importance. Well, I did get the ball rolling by giving another overview of the overall situation we found ourselves in, but since I would not be playing an active role in the negotiations, that was it as far as I was concerned. By then, I was starting to extemporize my introductions or talks, making them straight from the heart. On this occasion I ended my introduction by saying, "I wish you all satisfying and constructive negotiations." One of the trade union representatives reacted to this, saying that it was an odd thing to say, since I was one of the interested parties. I responded by saying that both parties were there to serve the staff interests and so everybody's interests were mutual. I then left the negotiating table. Naturally, I did follow the process.

It is unfortunate that trade unions operate according to a polarization model. It would be much better to take a joint approach. The "it, we and I model" is ideal for the purpose: the "it" side representing the financial side, the "we" side corporate culture and cooperative issues, and the "I" side the employees' personal development. To my mind, trade unions would achieve much more by bringing in these three perspectives in their dialogue with the company. It would, however, mean abandoning polarization as the perspective on reality from which both the employers and the unions operate.

The first round of negotiations was a kind of ritual dance. We reacted to the letters from the trade unions in which they set out their demands. Not only did CNV (*Christelijke Nederlandse Vakbeweging*, the National Federation of Christian Trade Unions) serve us with a list of demands, FNV (*Federatie van Nederlandse Vakbonden*, the Dutch Trade Union Federation) did too, even though they knew in advance that virtually everything would be rejected. It was already, in my eyes, one of the best organized collective labour agreements there were. Compared to those of other businesses, our collective labour agreement was gilt-edged.

After all of the unimportant little points had been rejected, we finally got down to the nitty-gritty: the salary increases that the process was really all about. The strategy was to make us feel, in advance, that – after all – they had already had to give up a lot. What with one thing or another, this part of the ritual dance lasted for about two negotiation rounds, and by this stage three weeks had passed. Notwithstanding the so-called Polder Model (the Dutch consensus-seeking model), there was a very traditional staking everything on salary increases. Our countermove was a fairly stingy salary offer: another predictable part of the ritual dance whose only result would be loss of time and possibly a feeling among the employees that the company was not as interested in their lot as was claimed. The bargaining process eventually reached its final phase. This time it was eight weeks after the start of negotiations. In summary form, the main section of the agreement – the salary section – went as follows:

- An offer of a 3.5% structural increase,
- 0.25% held in reserve for future cost increases associated with a new retirement plan,
- A creative bonus scheme linked to the uptime results.

The negotiations had ended up serving the short-term as well as the long-term interests of the employees. The short-term result was good because the structural increase of around 3.75% was high in terms of the collective wage agreements prevalent then (on average, collective wage agreements went no higher than 3.25%). The long-term result was good because there was an incentive for putting the focus on the whole uptime scheme, a scheme that was important for our future. What it boiled down to was that all of the employees could earn a one-off salary increase depending solely on the uptime results that were achieved: over a three-year period, approximately half of the financial gains produced via uptime would go into the pockets of the employees in the form of a one-off bonus. Everyone was happy with the document on the table. The trade unions, though, were not able in principle to sign the agreement until they had put the proposal to a meeting of their rank and file members. As they themselves put it, they would present the results in a neutral way but with positive undertones: language that I would find hard to use because it is not the language of the heart.

I was pleased, because we had been able to include the uptime results – so important for the company and our staff – as a financial stimulus. Our staff would profit financially from the results that were achieved. I was convinced that this collective labour agreement would go a long way towards helping people to play their part in making the uptime strategy work.

All of this took place towards the end of May, and up to this point it looked like a standard collective labour agreement process. It was, however, to take a surprising turn.

A couple of days later I opened my newspaper and, to my consternation, found an article on the collective labour agreement that we had come up with. My consternation had to do both with my feeling that a newspaper is no way of informing staff about their latest collective labour agreement and with the fact that, as usual, the newspaper had unfortunately made some careless errors in its reporting. Later in the same day, I asked myself whether we should not put something onto the cable TV bulletin board. We were not at liberty to do so, because it ran contrary to an age-old arrangement with the unions. As a company, we were not permitted to spread the news, because this could be regarded as undue influence. But wasn't one of our core values openness?

I was bothered by this, but since there was every indication that the proposal would be accepted that very week, I let the matter rest. A couple of employees within the company made a commotion about the fact that the newspaper had suggested that the agreement had already been reached. A similar misunderstanding the year previously had already antagonized some union members. Some assumed that the company had contacted the newspaper directly. I was able to put this notion to rest. It turned out to be a union representative who was keen to get into the newspapers.

On the Friday evening, I was quietly awaiting the results of the vote along with the Human Resources Director and the Manager of Employment Policy. Rank and file meetings of that kind are traditionally held in a local pub. We were telephoned with the news at about 8 pm: to our complete astonishment, the proposal had been rejected by both CNV and FNV. The *Unie (De Unie van Onafhankelijke Vakfederaties,* an independent general union) did, however, endorse the collective labour agreement proposal.

It later transpired that only 125 members of FNV and CNV had turned up to vote: about 10% of the members. Of them, 80% voted against. In other words, only 5% of the total membership voted against the collective labour agreement proposal, but threw everyone into a crisis. This was just how the system worked back then.

I was flabbergasted and quite emotional about it, to the extent even that, when I was alone in my office at 10 that evening, I even considered throwing in the towel. This organization just could not cope with its own good luck: since it already held a prime position, why would it bother choosing a course of lasting development? Blinded by success, greed, frustration, indifference, smugness and whatever else, it just wanted to fail.

I am lucky enough to have met a couple of people during my lifetime that I know I can always fall back on in good times as well as bad, and I now rang one of them. In my arrogance (an arrogance only heightened by my own emotional reaction), I felt that this organization just did not deserve my talents, and that it would not be difficult to find another organization that would be delighted to avail themselves of my insights. Fortunately, the person I rang that Friday evening made me see that it was right now that leadership was needed. It would be just too easy to give up now. Tired and angry, I went home.

In next day's newspaper there was an interview with me headed "A bestseller at Philip Morris". The article gave the main lines of how I viewed the changes to the corporate culture at Philip Morris and how well it was actually going. A small box in the middle of the article noted that the collective labour agreement proposal had been overwhelmingly voted out.

During the course of the weekend, I slowly regained my usual calm. Friday's emotional reaction was past and I certainly had no intention of resigning. I had decided to abstain from action: a different thing to not doing anything. Abstaining from action I describe as a state of being in which you are very alert to what is going on around you, but wherin you do not let yourself be tempted to act in ways that may seem logical but which are often ways of justifying your own ego or giving prominence to yourself. The situation I was in had nothing to do with myself as a person. The issue was how the organization could find a way out of the impasse that a small group of people had caused and which may have been a pretext for making a certain point. I did not want to turn it into a power struggle, because power struggles only produce losers, not winners.

It quickly became apparent that there were those who were prepared to take action to force a better collective wage agreement. There was even talk of going on strike. Various people advised me to start talking without any delay. The tide had to be turned, even if it meant mounting a soapbox. During the first week, I took the opportunity to tune into what was happening. My particular way of going about this is to listen, to observe and to try and put my finger on what the others are really concerned about. This was important to me: I did not want to act on the well-intentioned and reasonable advice that I had been given just yet. I did value the advice that I had been given, and it cannot have been easy for them to hear me reject it, as I did time and again.

A week later, the following things had become clear to me:
• A group of about 50 people were discontented.
• The discontent was a matter of old hurt, but also simple greed.
• Production was very good. A new record had even been reached.
• Most of the staff were not concerned about the collective wage agreement process.
• A number were baffled that the proposal had been rejected.
• Most, however, were relatively indifferent. I sensed that they did not care what really happened. So what if there was a bit extra in it for them? Things were bound to sort themselves out one way or another. There was no point in getting all worked up about it.

I ended my *Guust online* column by mentioning the fact that I had not been permitted to engage in any open dialogue relating to the collective wage agreement impasse. There were a lot of reactions to the column, including some from those who had voted against the collective wage agreement. I made a point of inviting some members of this group to the usual breakfast session two weeks after the conclusion of negotiations.

By the end of this breakfast session, I had obtained more respect for those who had actively voted, though not for the few negative types: the sort that you get in every organization. I view such people as rather sad and discontented types. They spend their working lives in a state of constant discontent, filled with a sort of destructive longing. It is unfortunate, but is their own choice. It was not these people that I gained a new appreciation of, but both those who were essentially well meaning but, because they had been misinformed in various ways, were barking up the wrong tree, and those who wanted to make a statement about some things that were not going well.

To my mind, the silent majority, who did not really care one way or another, formed the main problem: those who only reacted when it was too late, or who let others make their choices for them. They could even allow themselves the privilege of not voting. Then there were the hangers-on: those who always follow the leader. They will put aside any opinion they might have out of fear of not being accepted by the others. To one person they might say that they support the proposal but to others that they were absolutely right in not accepting things at all. You can only pity them.

We entered the third week. The unions had made an appointment to tell us officially that the negotiated agreement had been rejected and that they would come up with a new demand. We would have no option but to say that we had made our final offer: that that was all there was to it, and that the whole business would land in an impasse. The unions also asked our permission to hand out orange T-shirts to the employees on the eve of the discussions. These would be printed with a text that would give the discussions extra punch. Permission was granted, though I did put a notice on the cable TV bulletin board to the effect that we ought to stick to our core values and keep on treating each other with respect. I did not want to sow dissention merely on account of an orange shirt with the otherwise unoriginal text "NO means NO!"

A small group of people wore the shirt that day without causing too much commotion. In this matter too, I felt we had to remain in touch with the employees as much as possible. Those who were wearing the orange shirts would also retain my respect.

As was to be expected, the negotiations got completely bogged down that day. I decided then and there to give another personal rundown to those at the negotiating table on the uptime project and on the plans for initiating cultural change, as well as on its importance to the individual employees and its connection to the collective wage agreement. After a passionate speech, I tabled a new set of options. The proposed options were now either A (the collective wage agreement that had been rejected) or B: a collective wage agreement with a lower structural increase than in the rejected proposal but with a guaranteed and higher one-off payout. The B option sacrificed the (to my mind) important uptime bonus.

The unions eventually agreed to present the proposed options to their members and to hold a written ballot. They also requested that I give information about the proposal (including the context out of which the proposal ensued) to anyone who requested it internally. I was jubilant: I could finally talk to the staff!

The unions would also hold an informative meeting for their members. This would ensure that more than 100 employees were reached. I informed them that while I *was* prepared to give information on our proposal, I did *not* want to give how-to-vote instructions. In total, I held eight meetings of my own, which a total attendance of about 550 people. During those meetings, I made sure that I did not resort to bully tactics of the sort "No collective wage agreement? Then production will eventually end up in Third-World countries." I ended the series of meetings with the following comment: "It's now up to those employees who are a member of a trade union to vote. They will determine whether A or B goes ahead, or no collective wage agreement at all. Whatever their choice, I will respect it."

The written ballot produced an overwhelming majority for proposal A, the original proposal with the uptime bonus. It was a choice that the employees had made themselves. I mentally congratulated those who had let their voice be heard, who were critical, who asked questions, who were self-aware, and who dared to meet me and management face-to-face. The self-satisfied silent group had diminished somewhat in size.

I am glad that I did not give in to the threat of a strike or loss of face. I am glad that I was able to keep on meeting people face-to-face and to leave the choice to them.

The other option was the traditional path of persuading people and issuing threats: the path of compulsion. It is a path which will produce a collective wage agreement but will not bring the employees together. The organization will not undergo any development as a consequence, and so the next time around the language has to be even more persuasive and the threats even more menacing: a pointless and destructive path and one that has no intrinsic value.

■■■■■ **RECAP**

It takes quite a lot for a leader to be able to unite all the qualities that make him or her an all-round leader. To be able to combine empathy and clarity with the courage to make difficult and sometimes painful decisions is no simple task. You cannot do without any of these qualities, however.

To be honest about your real intentions and to accept others' opinions and expertise are not qualities that you often find represented in a single individual.

By now, you will have gathered that the path this developmental project took was not always strewn with roses. Good intentions do not necessarily always have the desired effect. You can be overwhelmed by matters that have nothing at all to do with what you are doing and which seem to be at cross purposes with what you want. "What on earth…! I didn't deserve this!" You are flabbergasted, you do not understand it at all, and you want to throw in the towel.

In such situations, it is tempting to focus on the issues involved. Instead, try and see how you can change your attitude: taking a different attitude can sometimes mean a different type of relationship, and consequently a discussion about different issues.

I do not know of any developmental project that is immune to this sort of thing. In retrospect, you may find yourself having a wry laugh about it, because you will have realized what the underlying deeper meaning was. But this will not help you when you are right in the middle of it all, when anger and despair are taking their toll of you. This is one such story.

In adverse circumstances such as these, it can indeed seem reasonable to enter the fray, to try and convince others of what you think and to stand up for what you believe in. In such cases, "standing up for" usually means "fighting for". This is precisely what did *not* happen here. Guust opted for abstaining from action, or more precisely for "not doing". It is an approach that needs some explanation. *Not doing* is not the same thing as *doing nothing*, and what is more, it is in a completely different category of things. As most people see it, you have two options open to you: either you work hard or you do nothing. Since the latter is not much appreciated by organizations, most people opt for working hard. You work hard at work, and when you get home or go on holidays you collapse and have to suffer the consequences: stress, breakdown, illness, burn-out, depression and, last but not least, the mid-life crisis.

Looking at it objectively, there is nothing wrong with hard work. What it boils down to is that hard work can either be an expression of yourself and what you regard as True, Good and Beautiful, or otherwise an expression of a kind of compulsion: you have to do it. That "having to do it" can come from within and derive from a norm such as having to do something useful with your life, or having to earn your livelihood the hard way. It can also come from the outside world, and be caused by external pressure exerted by your boss, the group, the organization, or the government. Whatever the case, it is compulsion and not a free choice – a choice you yourself have made. The issue at stake is discovering what you yourself want. If you work hard and experience working hard as the True, the Good and the Beautiful, this is quite a different thing from working hard because you have to.

Most people will identify with the second rather than the first. This is because we see ourselves as faced with a choice: the one option (working hard) is not as bad as the other (not doing anything). The choice is, in fact, a choice of two evils, and so we choose the lesser of the two.

What does this have to do with "not doing"? The whole point is that there is a third option. It is just not true that there are only two ways available: working hard versus doing nothing, or fighting versus surrendering, or winning versus losing, and so on. The other option is "not doing". It is a state of consciousness you see in, for example, samurai warriors and in some of the other Eastern martial arts. The warrior may to your eyes be standing motionless, but not only is he not working hard, he is not doing nothing either. He is not doing. He is quiet and alert, completely aware and on guard, but at the same time motionless and calm. All his senses are on full alert: he is ready to spring into action but without any inner pressure to do so, without "having to", and he is free from stress.

You also see it in the world of sports (golf, for example), and in the theater world: the actor who acts without it seeming to cost any effort. Simultaneously doing and not doing, the two held completely in balance. In the acting world, it is sometimes described as the neutral pose or, as a good friend once described it, as having the "let's see what happens now" mantra in your head.

In times like those described in the collective labour agreement tale, such an attitude will deliver the most lasting results. Not a militant "I'm going to teach them a lesson or two…" or an apathetic "let's just wait and see what happens next", but being there in a motionless state of activity, sometimes passionate, sometimes receptive.

It does help to keep the True, the Good and the Beautiful in mind. Combine them and they will put you into the "not doing" state. If you lose sight of any one of them, you will be back at square one. Keep a single one in mind and you'll remain alone.

"Come on, jump! We've got a good hold on you. Just jump!" A colleague was standing seven meters off the ground on a platform the size of a pizza. She had climbed up the pole and got onto the platform all by herself. She was, of course, attached to a rope, which was held tightly by eight colleagues. If she did fall, she would be hanging safely in the air. As soon as she reached the top, she was encouraged to jump from a height of seven meters into the void. With tears of terror in her eyes and knees shaking, she finally dared to jump. A second later and she was hanging in the air, a look on her face as though she had scorned death. She was then slowly lowered to earth. That evening, she was the heroine of the organization: such bravery!

This was part of a three-day course with the promising title "Create the Future" or CTF. It was a program that had blown over from America, along with a new American president. Its purpose was to demonstrate to the organization's top management that we could do more than we thought. What we had to do was get out of our comfort zone. It would seem obvious that the physical experience of leaping from a pole was not the same thing at all as leaving the safety of our "mental boxes", but nobody seemed to care very much. I saw quite a lot of people jumping that day. Some did it because it was an experience they just had to have had, but a lot jumped just because the others did. I wondered who had the greatest mental courage: those who jumped even though they did not really want to, or those who said that it was an experience they did not want and opted not to go along with the others. The program concluded with the request to everybody to ask their organization to try it out too. A number of my colleagues came up with the more or less unconvincing argument that now was not the right time for this: perhaps later (all the while hoping to shelve the idea). I was not very enthusiastic about the course either. I did, however, decide for it, though for a completely different reason.

Instead of experiencing it as a threat or something we just could not avoid choosing, I saw it as an opportunity to introduce a shortened version of our own Leadership Development Plan (LDP; see Chapter 15) into all levels of the company, up to and including the top management layer. I had already invited my boss to attend one of the international LDP courses, with the purpose of bringing him up to date with what we were doing in Holland. It was not hard to shift the focus of the course so that it also covered "Creating the Future". The issue was how to shift the commitment of the upper levels to the CTF course in order to obtain the resources we needed for our own LDP course.

Daniel, my boss, the American trainer of the "Create the Future" course and I spent an afternoon talking about how we could set up such a course. Getting approval took quite a bit of effort, but thanks to Daniel, his colleagues and a thorough preparation, we finally got the go-ahead. TDP (Team Development Program) was born.

Outside the Dutch borders, we simply called it "Create the Future". It was a tailor-made course created especially for the supervisor and his or her department. Its goal was to promote mutual cooperation in tackling the company's main strategy. Everything seemed to be going according to plan until the moment that our Human Resources Manager was giving a presentation on the contents of the course during an international Human Resources meeting. At the end of the presentation the then Vice-President of Western Europe came in. Technically, his authority did not extend to the factory at Bergen op Zoom, since his area was only Marketing and Sales.

He had only one question: "Is the pole in it?" The answer was no. The HR manager came up with numerous arguments, but to no avail. The pole just had to be in the program. We discussed the situation when we got back to the office. I realized that there was nothing to be gained by offering resistance. Being contrary never works. As I summed up the situation, resistance would only mean that the program would have to be altered even further. I decided to go along with things and slot the pole in somewhere, so that it caused the least amount of disturbance. I had no hesitation about doing this, because I had the feeling that the pole would not survive the course.

Before we knew it a seven-meter high pole had been erected in the Alexander Hotel in Noordwijk. The initial pilot course got under way in June and indeed, after the autumn evaluation the pole was taken down. Shortly after this, the Vice-President in question left the company. A coincidence? No way!

Compromising can sometimes be a good way of achieving your goal. A course that is 90% all right is better than no course at all. It is unfortunate, however, that some managers are more interested in externals and symbols (such as the exercise with the pole) than in the overall content.

The TDP course was a success, though as with any course, this would ultimately depend on what happened afterwards, once everybody was back in the daily grind. Its success was due to a number of factors:

1 Attendance was not compulsory. You will not get anything out of a participant who feels he or she has to attend.
2 Machines were to stop operating if necessary. This is a thorny issue in a production business. A number of departments did not want to go along with this and even proposed shuffling the groups around. We allowed this, but only as an exception. It was interesting to note that quite a number of groups came up with creative ways of preventing production being halted.

3 Whenever a new course started, I tried to explain what its purpose was whenever I had an opportunity to do so. There is no doubt that showing personal commitment is crucial to the success of any activity.
4 The groups were given the opportunity to give us – the management team – feedback. This feedback provided a lot of additional information in relation to corporate culture issues.
4 The matters discussed within the groups remained within the groups.
5 A shortage of professional guidance can pose a threat to in-company training sessions such as this. In addition to six trainers from Daniel's consultancy, we had thirty internal facilitators, who also became ambassadors for the proposed cultural changes.

TDP was able to reach the very core of a number of individuals. Although you could not express its success in financial terms, the course had had a greater effect than we had originally expected. The uptime project reached a new record. It is important, however, to keep on nurturing processes like these. You can do this by remaining alert, giving feedback and, if you see that it has a positive effect, by showing your appreciation. The results will automatically become more lasting.

██████ **RECAP**

This tale is about opportunities and choices. It is currently the "in" thing to be seeing where your boundaries lie and to leave your comfort zone, because doing so will arouse your creativity. It might, but it is by no means a certain thing. If you attempt to arouse your creativity by forcing yourself beyond your own boundaries, you will not arouse greater creativity, only a counter reaction. Force only leads to more force, even if you apply it to yourself. The issue is what you yourself want and choose, and whether what you choose is a creative or a reactionary choice, whether it is for or against something, whether it creates or is combative, whether it vitalizes you or wears you out. It is what you want that makes the difference between creativity or no creativity, not how much force is applied. While it is true that you need some tension to bring something into being, force and anxiety are not sustainable sources of energy. They might provide tension, but of a sort that tends to be destructive rather than creative.

Climbing up a pole says nothing about creativity, and so it had no place in the Team Development Program we envisaged. Moreover, the Dutch are just too down-to-earth to appreciate the funny side of such things. It certainly does match the notion that Americans get their kicks out of winning, and so conquering yourself, particularly things like fear and so on. If it is good for Americans, does this mean it is good for the world?

As Guust has said already, being contrary never works. What you lack in strength you have to make up for in cleverness: we managed to transform what seemed to be an obstacle so that it eventually became an ideal opportunity for obtaining the resources for an intensive course targeting 1,900 employees.

It is only when you know what it is that you want that you will be able to successfully transform setbacks and obstacles so that they become opportunities. The rule here, too, is never start by saying no, but by saying yes.

Both the content of the TDP course and the way it got underway were about who you are and what you want ("I"), seeing the opportunity ("it"), making creative choices ("I"), doing your homework properly ("it") and meeting people face-to-face ("we"). How the course came about was convincing proof that it really does work and does achieve results.

13 ACCEPTANCE

"What are your plans for Amstelveen and Brussels?" This was one of the first questions put to me on my being made responsible for the Benelux organization. The Benelux marketing and sales organization had merged several years previously, though it still had an office in Amstelveen and one in Brussels. The organization had been gradually converted into a united Benelux organization. For various reasons, however, the final step – bringing the two offices together in a single location – had not been made. When I took up my position and asked what stage things were at, it turned out that there were eleven possible scenarios in the files. It was unbelievable but true. Ultimately, there were only two possibilities open to us:

1 Leave everything as it was: an office in Brussels and one in Amstelveen.
2 Merge all of the activities.

The first option did not seem the most logical one, since at that stage about 60 people were traveling to and from Brussels on Monday and Tuesday, and then on Wednesday and Thursday changed to Amstelveen. On Friday, they were back at their "real" place of work: for some Brussels, for others Amstelveen. What this meant in real terms was that for nearly half the time, management was absent. It was no wonder that the theme of leadership was also brought up as an issue during the most recent work satisfaction investigation. Clearly, too, we could also economize further. The main advantage, however, lay in the opportunity to increase the organization's effectiveness. Faster decision-making, fewer communication breakdowns and a better focus on the consumers and customers. They were improvements that would be hard to measure in terms of figures, because they mainly derived from the interactive "we" area.

My initial move was to talk to everybody in the management team individually and ask them for their views, including what they stood to win or lose from the eventual decision.

By the end of the individual discussions everybody's personal stake had become quite clear. However, opinions on what had to be done now were quite diverse. I was struck by how well everyone managed to leave their own personal situation out of the main picture. My own personal preference was no secret to anybody. I hoped that this would not be taken as indicative of the final decision: this is not how I operate. But explain this to those who stood to lose their jobs or who would end up having to move...

The second step was to form a small team to perform an analysis. It was presented to the European management in the spring. The preferred scenario went as follows: both offices would be closed down and a new one set up in Antwerp. The economies that could be expressed in figures were fairly limited (the office staff could be reduced by 5%, and there would no longer be double rental and housing costs). The so-called soft economies could not be expressed in such terms and were barely discussed. The inefficient managerial traveling times were included via a simple calculation as a saving expressed in terms of man-days.

With one exception, the impact would be limited for those who lived in Brussels. They would be compensated for their additional traveling costs and, if they decided to move closer to the office, would have any moving costs refunded.
For those who lived in Amstelveen, the consequences would be great. I had insisted on guaranteeing the jobs of those who wanted to move. For those who did not or could not, there would be at least some solace in a severance scheme.

In mergers of this kind, the financial side (the "it" side) is usually taken care of adequately in our company. The emotional side, however, is often forgotten or dispensed with via a "good plan of communication". The challenge for me was to organize both sides as well as I could, thereby giving the employees a certain amount of time to take responsibility for their own affairs.

I announced the closure of the Amstelveen office to a meeting of the employees at the start of the summer. I gave a rundown of the considerations that prompted the decision and, of course, what the next steps were to be. Naturally, I did not expect full understanding among the staff, and indeed, their reactions varied from stunned amazement to anger, sadness, anxiety and resignation. The only thing that management could do during the period after the announcement was to make sure that we were there to listen to the staff and to the emotions they felt. I will always remember Belinda, one of the administrative staff, telling me straight after the announcement that she was terribly angry and just did not want to speak to me right then. Her personal circumstances were particularly difficult and it would not be easy for her to find a new job. Her reaction was a genuine one, and I could understand it. Just a few days later Belinda turned up during the coffee break. I listened to what she had to say. There was little more I could do than demonstrate understanding for her situation and indicate what the next steps were going to be.

After they are confronted with bad news, people undergo a phase of denial, anger and/or anxiety. This is completely normal. The important thing is to remain in touch, to just be there. Do not try to talk their emotions away, but allow them the space to go about dealing with their emotions at their own pace. As soon as they have gone through the rough times, they will reach a stage of seeing new options and opportunities. Only then, the future will take on any brightness for them.

A month further into the summer saw the signing of a severance deal with the unions. It was a deal which, in addition to the good severance arrangement, provided an excellent outplacement scheme. In addition, everybody was given until the first of November to choose what they wanted to do: move to Antwerp too or accept the severance deal. The ensuing period was one of vacillation and many sleepless nights. Belinda came by regularly for a quick coffee break. Like many others, she was slowly getting on top of her life again. She was an inspiration to many in the same situation, since everybody knew of her personal circumstances: if she could rise to the occasion, who couldn't?

During the July to November period there were also some "threats" in the form of suggestions that nobody would move to Antwerp. They were understandable in their own way, but what I could not accept was that, subconsciously, it was putting those who did want to move under pressure to make a different decision after all. I wanted everybody to be free to make their own decisions. The best way of going about this was by listening and particularly by avoiding trying to twist others' arms. Being there and giving honest answers to any questions was management's only obligation. It was easier for some than for others. Those who want to derive profit from such situations must also be dealt with clearly. They are inclined to negotiate every little thing, from their mobile phone and their car during the outplacement period up to and including farewell parties. Belinda was not part of this: she had worries of her own.

"One-third will move to Antwerp," announced the Personnel Director. I could accept this because I had the impression that virtually everyone's decision had been freely and consciously made. Now we were free to start designing the new organizational structure. Since we had set no targets, management was also free to put all its available energy into it and to create a made-to-measure product.

In the meantime, we had found out that we could move into our new quarters in Antwerp much earlier than we had anticipated: in the coming January instead of in August. We could now take the plunge: the sooner we moved to Antwerp and could begin merging the two offices the better, not only for the new organization but also for those who would stay behind, since they could start working on their new futures sooner. The office was opened in the second week of January, which also saw the unveiling of the new organizational structure. A small group stayed behind at Amstelveen to finish off any remaining business.

A year later, we made up the balance:

1 Virtually everybody who decided not to move had in the meantime found a new job. Belinda had too. Her strong character and the fact that she had refused to play the victim made this possible. Despite all the support that the company had given them, only one or two had not survived the process well. It was unfortunate but unavoidable when there are other issues playing a contributing role. The company can do little in such circumstances: nothing you do will be any good. As a leader, you have to draw your own boundaries, though only after you have reached the conclusion that you have done everything you could.

2 The eventual economies turned out to be much greater than expected. Instead of economizing on 5% of the total staff numbers, it turned out to be 20%.

3 The business suffered hardly any interruption to its processes. The move caused hardly any problems for suppliers, customers or our clients in the field.

4 The merger of the two offices could be described as a success a mere year after moving into our new Antwerp office. I have rarely witnessed such an enthusiastic end-of-year seminar as the one that year. Regardless of who they were or where they came from, the members of the organization were filled with a true team spirit.

Each meeting room at our new Antwerp offices is named after one of our core values: Respect, Integrity, Transparency and Passion. The big meeting room is called Inclusiveness. Believe me, they were never as bubbling over with life as they were during that end-of-year seminar!

RECAP

This was an almost copy-book description of a reorganization. Guust's predecessor, however, apparently found it too hard to break the ties that were holding the organization back. The tale reminded me of a conversation that I once had with Frits Philips about values and organizations. When I asked him whether he could reconcile a moral approach to work with making painful decisions perhaps involving hundreds of people being fired, he gave the following lucid answer:

If you can keep in touch with what your decisions mean for people, you can maintain your integrity and trustworthiness. It's a matter of keeping in touch with your feelings. Decisions like these are very painful for anybody who stands to lose their jobs and for their families. While the decision will have been made on sensible grounds, this doesn't mean that you have to divorce yourself from your feelings. Many managers just can't manage this, however.

Feeling isn't an expression of pity: it's an expression of compassion, even though all the while you know it isn't much help to those people. What you have to learn to do is accept the following things:
1. *That you can't ease their pain,*
2. *That you probably can't help them,*
3. *That your feelings are yours alone, and others will be inclined to experience them as hypocritical,*
4. *That their pain will sometimes be directed at you in the form of anger,*
5. *That you can't do anything about this either.*

The key word here is "acceptance".

In this account of a merger, acceptance started with taking on the responsibility of breaking ties, and doing so on the basis of "it", "we" and "I" considerations: weighing up how true, how good and how beautiful the factors that play a role in the decision were.

Guust was only able to influence the process of integration that followed to a limited degree. Acceptance of relative powerlessness is, however, not as easy as it seems. Acceptance is sometimes confused with a resigned attitude: "I can't do anything about it, so there's no point in identifying with how others feel." A consequence is that you divorce yourself from your feelings and sever your "I" from the process. Acceptance means staying in there; resignation means denying yourself the process of dealing with your emotions. The main point is that it is not only a matter of the "victims" dealing with their emotions, but of acceptance that you – the person who carries the main responsibility – are part and parcel of the process.

An organic approach to mergers increases the chance of their taking place smoothly, though it is no guarantee. What does strike me, however, is that taking an organic approach means that you as the one in charge will end up with a different result from that which you would have had if you had taken a one-sided (or severed) "it", "we" or "I" approach. You could call this coincidence, but I have experienced too many coincidences to attribute it to coincidence alone.

That you do not have to accept everything unquestioningly will have become apparent from the story. If you (as the one in charge) have an insight into your own way of dealing with your emotions, this will make it easier to decide what you want to accept and what not.

"To be accepting inside is to have strength outside" would be an appropriate motto for this sort of process.

PART III
THE COMPONENTS

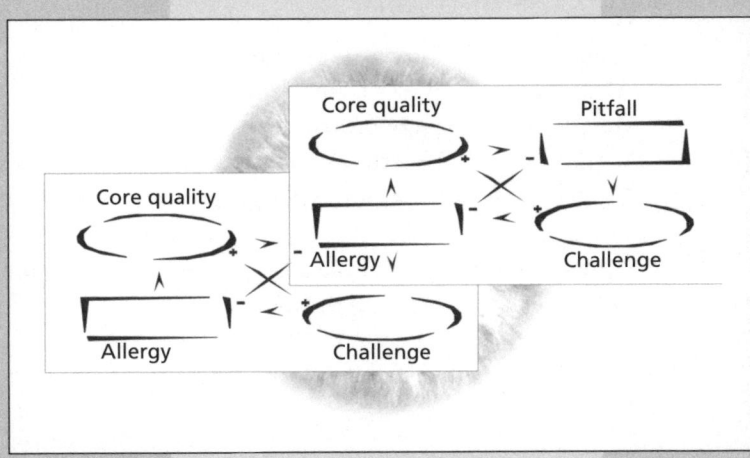

14 A CHRONOLOGICAL OVERVIEW OF THE PHILIP MORRIS HOLLAND DEVELOPMENTAL PROJECT

Year 1

February	Start of the LDP pilot study
September	Start of COM (Career on the Move) pilot study

Year 2

January	First management session (under the leadership of Guust's predecessor)
May	Second management session (under Guust's leadership)
July	The first Culture Club session
October	Third session with the management team
November	The second Culture Club session
December	The first session with Culture Club 2

Year 3

January	*Gemba* gets underway
February	Start of the reintegration pilot study
March	Second session with Culture Club 2
April	Fourth session with the management team
August	Initiation and first meeting of the management team
September	Start of the STOK project: integration policy
December	Meeting in Gent

Year 4

January	*Creating the Future* meeting in Barcelona (Philip Morris International)
February	The second group management meeting
March	First *Guust Online*
April	Collective labour agreement negotiations
May	The third group management meeting
June	TPD (Team Development Program) pilot study course for 1,900 employees
September	The fourth group management meeting in Les Piglais (France)

Year 5

May	The last TDP course
June	The fifth group management meeting

15
THE LDP/COM/TDP LEADERSHIP AND DEVELOPMENT COURSES

The ideas that we described earlier – namely, the Leadership Development Program (LDP), the Career on the Move (COM) program and the Team Development Program (TDP) – were introduced in full during a period of five years via three training courses that ran the full length of the course.

The Leadership Development Program (LDP) grew out of the question that started the whole process: how could we learn to deal with our feelings better? The question was quickly translated into a leadership development issue and was taken up by the Human Relations Director. At that stage, Guust was responsible for production.

This course was targeted at middle management (all managerial staff above the supervisor level). Its success and the enthusiasm the course aroused quickly led to the development of the Career on the Move (COM) program, targeting those who wanted to take bearings on their careers and to see whether they lay inside or outside the company. These courses culminated in a very extensive course: the Team Development Program (TDP), which targeted all of the 1,900 employees, with a special role for supervisors. All in all, they required an enormous amount of effort and asked a lot of the organization.

LDP (Leadership Development Program)
Ultimately, the LDP owed its beginnings to the following. Philip Morris at Bergen op Zoom had witnessed ongoing growth for years. Increasing internal competition made it likely that this growth would

level out or even stop in the foreseeable future. This development had not gone unnoticed, and required those at all managerial levels to set their aims higher. As the largest branch in Europe, it needed to set an example for the other branches within the company. In the past, trials had been done with self-directed teams. Total Quality Management was implemented and management had done a training session in efficient managing. The activities had focused particularly on technology and the approach was a how-to-use-it one (a typical "it" approach taken by many management courses).

The upshot was that there was now a call for a follow-up course for senior staff who fell outside the collective labour agreement. This course would contribute to the development of those in managerial positions and help them to function successfully now and in the future. The theme would be the development of personal qualities.

For a period of about six months, the course participants (arranged in groups of a minimum of twelve and a maximum of sixteen) worked towards a concrete goal: perceptible behavioural changes. To get into the course, the participants needed to have an individual PDP (Personal Development Plan) entry interview with the external group leader prior to the commencement of the course. The participant's personal goal was established during the course of this interview and, during the course itself, the course supervisor repeatedly stressed the importance of translating the program into practical results and individual performance.

The program was drawn up in such a way as to preclude lack of commitment. It consisted of two parts:

1 the training program,
2 a feedback group.

During the intervening feedback sessions the participants worked on the development of skills and increasing their perception of themselves and of how they were performing ("I" and "we").

During the interim period, the participants worked in small groups giving themselves feedback based on assignments that they did as homework. During these sessions, the groups devoted some time to discussing how to put theory – the things that had come out of the training program – into practice.

The program's content revolved around five themes:
- Leadership and the core values,
- From compulsion (having to) to desire (wanting to) to choice (choosing to),
- Communication and creativity,
- Managing fear and learning trust,
- Entrepreneurship and perseverance,
- How to exert an influence on the corporate culture (collective behaviour).

The training program consisted of three units of about three days each. Each unit had three recurring themes:

1 The central themes of each individual unit
The five themes mentioned above formed the basis and were treated in conjunction with each other. They dealt with awareness and insight as well as skills, behaviour and techniques ("it", "we" and "I").

2 Relaxation and effort
This had as its goal introducing participants to relaxation and movement techniques. The participants would learn to put their daily routine to one side and to bring clarity to their thoughts by trying out various techniques that would be explained and demonstrated. One technique or way of encouraging inspiration or concentration would be introduced in each unit.

3 Putting it into practice

At the end of each unit, a move was made to translate theory into practice, usually in the form of an assignment that could be done within the individual work situation or within the feedback groups.

The three units dealt with the following subjects:

Unit 1 Who are you and what do you want?

The objective of this unit was to develop individual awareness of what the participants wanted in terms of their own personal development as well as in their capacity as managers. It also focused on each participant's core qualities in conjunction with their leadership. The focus was largely an "I" focus.

I   "Passion and Quality in People and Organizations" (introduction).

What is it that makes people want to join in or not?

How do you discover and develop your own core qualities and those of others (introduction, practice exercise and game)?

"From Compulsion to Desire to Choice" (introduction, exercise and practice, and test). How can you develop your own sense of commitment and that of others? How do you draw up your own priorities? What implications does this have for how you manage others? What is the difference between acceptance and resignation?

II "Relaxation and effort" (aikido).

Letting your body itself tell you whether you are being reactive, responsive or creative. When are you in balance and when out of balance? The objective is to experience in physical form the principles and concepts previously introduced.

III Putting it into practice (to be based on individual situations).

The following were on the agenda:
- What do I want? What are my goals?
- Where does my strength lie?

- How do I make it work?
- How can I recognize my own core qualities?
- What choices am I making and why?
- How do I learn to make effective choices?

Unit 2 How do you make it all work?

The objective of this unit was to enhance the ability of the participants to communicate effectively and to deal flexibly with each other. The participants were shown techniques aimed at giving them an insight into how they usually acted and shown ways of changing this, and of practicing how to go about it. It also focused on communicating and improvising in creative ways. The accent here was on the I and the Other.

I   Forms of communication.
Communication can take many forms. When can it be described as effective? How can you expand your repertoire of communicative methods? When are you being open to others and when not?

II Relaxation and effort (drama improvisation).
Learning to deal with anxiety using physical techniques. The objective is to learn how to play and to improvise in the way you do things.

III Putting it into practice.

The following were on the agenda:
- What am I saying and what do I want to say?
- How can I use my voice, my body and other non-verbal techniques?
- How do I come across to others and how do I deal with their reactions?
- How can I prepare myself for a conversation that could be difficult?
- Improvisational techniques.

Unit 3 How can you ensure that the corporate culture stays the way you want it?

The objective of this unit was to enhance the participants' insights into departmental and corporate cultures and ways of dealing with these cultures. The accent here was obviously on the "we" side.

I   Corporate culture and analyzing it (an introduction and exercise directed at charting company customs that have become ingrained).

Drawing up an outline of the desired corporate culture.

Drawing up a plan of development directed at achieving the desired culture within the department.

II Relaxation and effort.

Martial arts.

III Putting it into practice.

Filling in an IDP (Individual Development Plan).

The following were on the agenda:
• How do you hone a culture?
• How do you coach people to conform to a culture?

Personal coaching

The role of coach was filled by one of the two trainers. This role was seen as an essential part of the program. The coach's task was to coach the participants individually during the various units. The coach would establish jointly with the participant what his or her goals for the course were and use these goals in giving any feedback necessary in order to achieve the desired change in behaviour.

The feedback groups

Feedback groups (PDP groups) were formed in the period between the various course units. The participants worked in small groups under the supervision of the course supervisor on homework tasks which had to do with the preceding unit. These groups allowed the participants to acquire some interim practical knowledge and experience relating to what they had learned in the previous unit and to exchange experiences.

We can say without any equivocation at all that that this course was an outstanding success. The evaluation scores were the highest in the history of Philip Morris and the participants were very enthusiastic right from the start. The comment most overheard was without any doubt: "If only our bosses thought this way and did these things."

Because it was originally a course for middle management, there were no plans at that particular moment to start work at the directorial level of management. This did entail a risk: the risk that the "language" learned would remain restricted to middle management and that the gap between the two levels would only increase. It was precisely at that crucial moment that Guust was appointed General Director, and the directorial level started to be actively involved. The timing could not have been better!

COM (Career on the Move)

A number of the LDP components were very suitable for use with other target groups. As part of the Philip Morris International, Philip Morris Holland had been growing steadily since the early 1980s. A large proportion of the staff of 1,900 had by this stage been with the company for a long time. Commitment and loyalty were high. Philip Morris recognized the importance of having independent employees who were taking responsibility for their own development. It wanted to encourage the staff to continue this way by offering them the opportunity to focus voluntarily on their own development to an even greater degree. COM's objective was to support employees in their efforts to raise their level of commitment. The statement was: "Employees who are aware of what they can offer and try to put their talents to optimal use within Philip Morris are valued human resources."

Correspondingly, the COM objectives were as follows:
• To make the employee even more aware of his or her qualities and what he or she has to offer.

- To give employees the ways and means they need to give direction to their career.
- To encourage the employee to take responsibility for his or her career.

The workshop's agenda revolved around three questions that one way or another informed the two-day session.
- What point are you at in your working life and what are you putting into it in terms of your capabilities?
- What else do you want to do in your life (whether in your working life or otherwise)?
- How can you achieve this?

The course was based on having a maximum of 10 participants. It took up two consecutive days plus one additional day at a later date.

Day 1
What point are you at in your working life and what are you putting into it?
    Team qualities,
    Core qualities,
    Simulation exercise.

Day 2
How can I achieve what I want?
    "Wanting to" versus "choosing to",
    Various ways (individual, group) of interpreting an employee's wishes and of fulfilling them.

This course was also received enthusiastically and resulted in a lot of staff members coming up with new initiatives, varying from starting a course of training to looking for a new job.

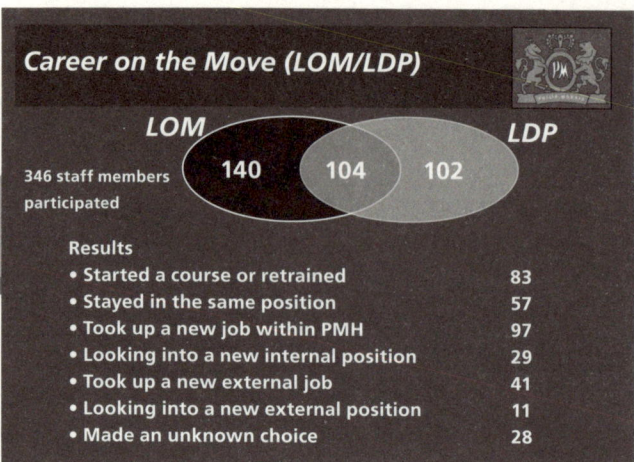

The illustration (Figure 27) shows what the course had achieved three years later. Not only were the tangible ("it") results striking, there was an equivalent impact on the organization ("we"). A survey of work satisfaction demonstrated that, within two years, the score had risen from 6.2 to 7.6.

Results

- Work satisfaction investigation
  Valued the experience of working for PMH
  4 years later   7.6%
  Was previously   6.2%

- Absenteeism due to illness
  4 years later   4.0%
  Was previously   5.1%

- Midspeed uptime
  4 years later   69%
  Was previously   60%

Naturally, this cannot be solely attributed to the course, but it certainly played a role.

The main effect was, however, that working styles became more human as a result, or rather, became organic. Although the business originally had a typical "it" flavour, it turned into one with traces of an organic approach.

TDP (Team Development Program)

The Team Development Program (TDP), which everyone within the company participated in, was by far the most comprehensive of the courses. This ambitious project took an immense amount of company effort, involving 1,800 people becoming acquainted with the ideas behind the project as a whole in more than 140 two-day workshops spread over a period of nine months. These ideas were part of the LDP, adapted to fit the actual situation of the team in question. What it boiled down to was that every team had an individualized TDP session. The program sometimes differed greatly from others, each being examined and adapted by the facilitators' team and the supervisors on a session-by-session basis.

The logistics alone made it a massive operation, since on occasion the courses took place in Noordwijk, while the factory was in Bergen op Zoom. The experiences that were had during those TDP sessions could fill a book in their own right.

16 TRANSITIONAL PROCESSES AND PAIN

Talking about the "nice" things in life is not a particularly challenging developmental course activity. When things are going pretty smoothly within the organization, it is relatively likely that the interactions will be superficial and will not be given much of a chance to gain any depth. Things only get serious when the going gets tough, when there are setbacks, and when big changes are afoot and things no longer seem so assured. Making a team, a departmental or a project group breakthrough is often accompanied by pain. Transitions are rarely "nice", let alone inspirational.

When pain became an acceptable topic within a team, often something very special happened. Artifice and superficiality would fall away and we would find ourselves confronted with life's realities. As soon as individual vulnerability – the vulnerability of the "I" – manifested itself within the organization and was allowed to remain, the atmosphere (the "we") automatically opened up and "it" topics where discussed in a different way in our discussions. Things calmed down, people listened more, there was more attention paid and opportunities suddenly opened up: we could just do more, even if they were "it" things. People became more creative, because they could be themselves, could show all their sides and were less inclined to be guided by their "have to" selves. Pain turned out to be a miraculous doorway to being more rounded people.

Because we do cause each other pain – often without wanting to do so – it is very important that we be able to talk about it. Opportunities to talk about our pain were often readily available to us (not surprisingly when you realize that we are surrounded by it). It was a matter of being open to it and it would be there. Sometimes it was a personal tragedy in a team member's life, sometimes a rather too humorous comment made to another: a comment which you sensed had hit home. On one occasion it was an air disaster involving a Swissair plane in which a number of colleagues were killed. It could be major pain, it could be minor pain.

While pain is a taboo topic for the "it" side of things, for the "I" side it is almost everyday reality. A colleague being treated without respect by someone in a managerial position will hurt you. This may seem a bit obvious, but many will not even feel it because it will almost instantaneously be masked by anger or fear. It is virtually impossible to express fear or anger of this sort in an environment lacking in respect and values: the atmosphere will be too perilous, the surroundings too harsh. The result will be that both the fear and the anger will be suppressed, with cynicism taking their place. There is quite a chance that under the same leadership, this cynicism will arouse an even greater lack of respect, and a vicious circle will have been created.

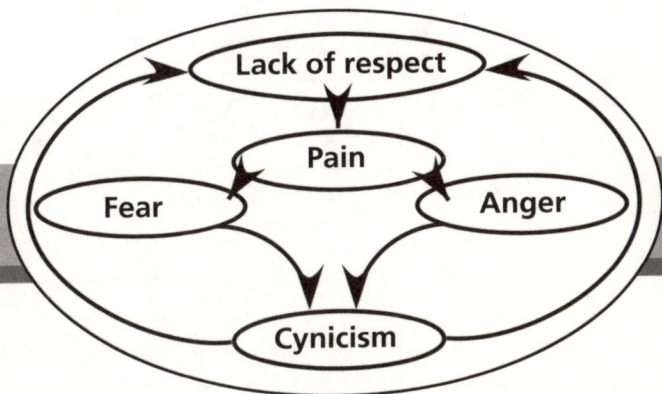

The vicious circle created by management that is lacking in respect

It is important to realize that with a vicious circle of this sort, every expression of cynicism represents pain that is masked, and this pain needs to be handled with sensitivity. This is no easy brief, because the chance is great that even a sensitive approach will initially be met with cynicism. To maintain it will require some perseverance, therefore.

In situations like these, the important thing is to realize that as soon as you elect to take a respectful approach, you may be inclined to assume that this will eliminate all the pain. This is not so. People will cause each other pain even in organizations where values inform the way that people operate. It may not be intentional, but that is neither here nor there. The real difference is that the anger or fear – which will still be present – is hopefully allowed and may be expressed. It will no longer have to be disguised as cynicism: sadness will replace it. This is a prerequisite for dealing with pain and it will lead to acceptance, a source of nourishment for respect.

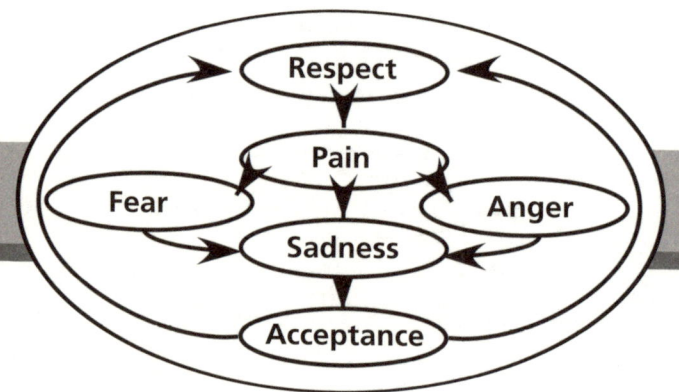

The cyclic development that management can initiate by showing respect

Organizations that are driven by their values are few and far between, not because there is a dearth of leaders who want to base their actions on values, but because there are few leaders who are capable of integrating "we" values (Goodness) with Truth ("it") and Beauty ("I").

Becoming aware of core qualities was an essential aspect of the project as a whole. All of the individual courses devoted some attention to this. Without going into the theory of core quadrants at any length, the following overview shows how much the theory was able to contribute.

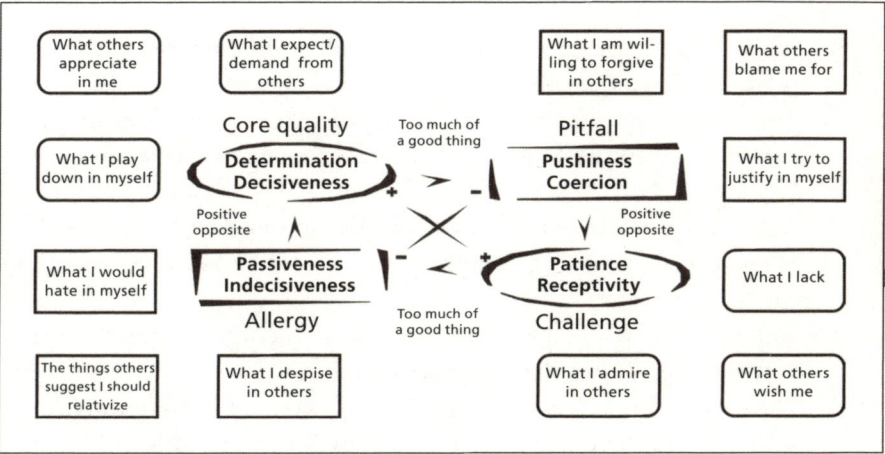

The illustration summarizes the twelve points of entry you can take to obtain an insight into all of the aspects of the core quadrant at both the individual ("I") and collective levels ("we").

They will produce the following 25 insights:

1 Your core quality can be defined as the quality that others experience as inspiring and which only requires you to be aware of. You do not have to do anything to have it. Your core quality is always there and always at your disposal. You can always fall back on it.

2 Core qualities lend colour to your personality, to the way you act, to your skills and to the way you view the world.

3 You have the tendency to take your core qualities for granted, and even to denigrate them: "What's so special about that?"

4 Your weak point (you could call it your "pitfall") is over-reliance on your core quality: too much of a good thing. They are part and parcel of each other.

5 Your weak point is often what others reproach you for or label you as: "Don't be so…".

6 You will be inclined to dismiss your weak point as minor: "It's not as bad as all that…"

7 The things that you do not like in others are consequently no more than their weak points, and thus over-reliance on their core qualities.

8 Your personal challenge is the positive opposite to your weak point. Your personal challenge is what you have to develop within yourself.

9 Your personal challenge will almost always be what you admire in others or even what attracts you to others.

10 The main thing is not to get rid of your weak point but to complement your core quality by rising to your personal challenge.

11 As such, you do not have to have less of something (i.e., of your weak point) or to forfeit something (i.e., your core quality), but to add something (i.e., your personal challenge).

12 Consequently, you should not concern yourself with what you *do not* want (your weak point), but with what you *do* want (your personal challenge).

13 It is not a matter of either deploying your core quality or rising to your personal challenge, but of doing both simultaneously: not an "either or" but an "and and".

14 Being in balance is a matter of integrating core qualities and challenges within yourself.

15 The things that provoke an "allergic" reaction in you represent the things you find too challenging: they are diametrically opposed to your core quality.

16 Your weak point is not the problem: but the allergic reaction is, since it is your dislike of your allergic reactions that your weakness arouses.

17 Your condemnation or even distain of your allergic reactions is what stymies you, since it arouses your weakness.

18 The advantage of an allergic reaction is that it will provoke you into sending out your feelers and so to pick up the things that are going on, and do something constructive with them.

19 When you are under pressure or in stressful situations, you will fall back on your weak point and even subsequently resort to allergic reactions.

20 You can learn the most from those you react to most strongly. This is because they have too much of the quality you need more of.

21 People are not bad. Negativity results from lack of awareness, from not noticing things.

22 The chance is great that your life partner's or best friend's core quality is your personal challenge.

23 Consequently, you are probably wedded to that which you react most strongly to, though this will usually only have become apparent to you after the honeymoon was over.

24 Your allergic reactions will usually have a comparatively stronger pull on you than your personal challenge will attract you, and, until you stop thinking that the two are virtually synonymous, you will never rise to your challenge.

25 When the other's weak point is what you react to most strongly, there will be a very real threat of conflict.

If 2,000 people each arrive at these 25 insights at both the personal level and at the level of their interaction with others, the resulting 50,000 insights can reasonably be expected to provoke a cultural change.

This calculation is, of course, a highly exaggerated one, the typical twisted logic of an "it" thinker, but we hope that we have convinced you that via the LDP, COM and TDP courses, something certainly did take place collectively within the organization as the staff became acquainted across the board with this low-threshold way of looking at "I" and "we" issues. Replace the words "you" and "your" with the words "we" and "our" and you have 25 new insights, this time within the domain of the "we". Individual core quadrants will turn into collective cultural quadrants and you will be describing the organizational culture and interactions in the same language. Couched in "I" terms, our quest is for Beauty in each individual; in "we" terms, we can now enter into a dialogue (a different thing to starting a discussion) on the subject of Goodness.

The core quadrant was able to produce an "I" language and a "we" language: the organization had started to become multilingual. As with every language, if you do not speak it for a while you lose your command of it. That happened too, but not before 1,900 CD-ROMs of that language had been handed out, a total of 140 "language" courses given, and a number of instructors trained.

COMMITMENT 18

What a misused word it is, the word "commitment". It is most misused by the boss who says, "But we've committed ourselves, and so we have to…", because in that one small sentence are two inaccuracies:

1 "We" did not commit ourselves: it was an individual choice.
2 You do not "have to" do anything at all, not even if you have committed yourself to something!

Most people would want some clarification here, and this is why these issues formed a major part of the developmental project within Philip Morris. They fell under the heading of "From compulsion ('having to') to desire ('wanting to') to choice ('choosing to')". A lot of people think they are being creative when what they are actually doing is trying out this and that: a different thing altogether. This topic got to the very heart of the project as a whole, because it reached the essence of the concept of creativity and was an excellent way of teaching both organic ways of thinking and how to focus on getting results.

The main issue is that of how to realize your desires: how you can really make a success of the things you want to achieve. From another angle, how can you as a manager and as a person create what you want? The problem is rarely not wanting something enough. The problem is that we cannot *choose*! If you listen closely to someone who wants something, you will almost inevitably detect an "if" behind what he or she is saying: "I'd like that… if I had the ways and means… if I had the staff… if I had the time… if it had the support of my wife…", and so on. Since these will usually be conditions that are virtually impossible to fulfill, you can bet that the person in question will turn up three weeks later to tell you why it did not work. It is not that he did not *want* it enough, but because he had not chosen to do it. He probably still wants it!

Making changes or achieving results has little to do with merely being prepared to give it a go. Good intentions are not sufficient to achieve results. Merely being prepared to give something a go already has a built-in failure clause and is not conducive to getting up the energy that you need to achieve it. To put it another way: *wanting* something is the spark that gets you going; *choosing* something from your very heart is the fuel you need to get results. Failure to get what you want is often blamed on something external to the person: on circumstances or on another person. In a way you are saying, "I can't help it." By doing this, you are declaring that you lack power. Powerlessness is the source of a lot of unnecessary misery within organizations. It is behind stress-related and time management problems, and behind many illnesses and lack of energy.

> *People do not get sick from working too hard,*
> *but they do from pointlessness and powerlessness.*

As mentioned above, the secret of creativity is making choices. This is what commitment really is: an inner and binding choice, made freely and not because one *has to*. It is an individual process, therefore, and not a collective one. *We* don't choose, the individual chooses.

The process of achieving one's desires can be split up into six steps[1]:
1 Listening closely to what you really want,
2 Focusing your energy on achieving tangible results,
3 Focusing closely on the things that are objectively real at the current moment,
4 Checking whether your choice is going to be an effective one,

---

[1] Each of these steps is described in detail in *Core Qualities: a Gateway to Human Resources*, Daniel Ofman, published by Scriptum Publishers, ISBN 90 5594 240 5.

5 In the light of 4, choosing what you want to achieve,
6 Following what happens and letting go.

None of these steps must be overlooked. Doing so will almost inevitably lead to ineffective choices that will not really provide the desired results.

Step 4 – checking the likely effectiveness of your choice – deserves particular mention. Any choice should be subject to an effectiveness check. Ineffective choices are choices which create a new reality but not the one that you had in mind. They will thus provide no satisfaction and you will be disappointed in them. There are seven checks that you can carry out to increase the chances of the choices turning out to be effective ones. They are as follows:

- A check on how creative the choices are,
- A check on what they can be expected to contribute,
- A check on how imbedded they are within the organization,
- A check on whether they are unconditional,
- A check on whether they are within your area of responsibility,
- A check on their ramifications,
- A check on their inclusiveness.

The most important effectiveness check you can carry out is on *creativity* versus *reactivity*. Is it a choice for or against something? Will I be creating something with it or avoiding or destroying something with it? Effective choices are always for something, not against something. This notion corresponds to insights 10, 11 and 12 of the core quadrants: not focusing on what you want to be rid of (your weak point) but on what you can contribute (your personal challenge).

The second check is on whether the effects can be expected to contribute to the bigger picture: to the organization that I am a member of, for example, or to my family or society.

The third check is a check on how imbedded the chosen action is in the whole. It goes without saying that some choices are more crucial than others. The more imbedded in the structure as a whole, the greater the effect. Every decision to back something up is to a certain extent a confirmation of an elementary decision, and hopefully an essential one.

The fourth check is on whether the choice is unconditional. The question is whether there are any conditions attached and, if so, what they are. "I choose to finish this task today if my secretary can make sure that I am not disturbed" is not a choice but a wish. Such conditional choices undermine one's creative power enormously. As mentioned above, they are not about creating but about trying things out.

The fifth check on effectiveness is a check on operational capacity. If the choice involves another person, you will have to step outside your own immediate sphere of operation and consequently outside the area for which you hold responsibility.

The sixth check is on the ramifications of the choice. Asking yourself the question "If I could have it, would I want it?" may seem pointless. Nevertheless, many people would get the fright of their lives if they were granted their wish. Since you can assume that, having made a choice, you will be confronted with its effects, it would seem wise to make sure that the results will please you.

The final check – on inclusiveness – may to some extent overlap the previous checks, but is so important that it is better to do it double than to run the risk of overlooking it. Exclusive choices provoke reactions and trouble and will turn out not to have been good ones. One could imagine any number of choices of an exclusive kind which have the potential to have disastrous effects. Eliminating competitors, for example. Despite this, many people are more comfortable with the idea of eliminating an opponent than they are with enlisting an associate (the *aikido* ideal).

To include others has nothing to do with being a nice person. Not only that, but clear boundaries, clarity of thought and even coming over as a tough opponent are also manifestations of thinking in terms of inclusiveness. What is important is the intention. In other words, the ultimate check on effectiveness is the check on inclusiveness.

A step-by-step approach to turning your desires into choices will increase your chances of success. This is because the approach is an organic one: looking at the world from all angles. Learning to make choices is consequently an exercise in learning to think holistically.

19 CULTURAL ANALYSIS

Analyses of the corporate culture are another tool of the trade. A cultural analysis is just a means of initiating a dialogue on customs and habits. Included below is a list of contentions that were put to the various groups. The resultant scores (which were presented in the form of a profile) formed little more than a pretext for a discussion on them. The value of this kind of tool does not lie in scores but in the discussion the scores give rise to. It is a typical "it"-style tool: if you did not have your wits about you, you could be fooled into thinking that it had some objectivity to it, objectivity that might prompt an "it" manager to draw up a plan and circulate it – a monologue of sorts – within the organization. Our primary interest was not in drawing up a plan but in initiating a dialogue. For interest sake, we sometimes included the results in the LDP, COM and TDP courses.

Drawing up a cultural quadrant was an alternative to lists of contentions. As soon as the participants had learned how to apply the language of the core quadrants to their own personal development, they could take this step in their stride, applying the "I" language to the "we" side of things. Both approaches made a useful contribution to opening up for discussion matters relating to culture, collective behaviour, customs and habits, interactions, manners, and so on.

The following is a list of contentions used for the purpose of arousing discussion:

In my opinion, it is customary in Philip Morris

I   Outlook/mission
+   for management to clearly indicate the things we stand for,
+   to take the long-term view into account in our daily comings and goings,
+   for management to regularly tell us what our mission and outlook is,
−   to react in an ad hoc way to any changes.

II   Managerial consistency
−   for the various managers to decide independently of the others in what way his/her staff will be involved in the department's/group's well-being,
+   for management to be consistent in evaluating staff performance,
+   for management to take a uniform approach in drawing the attention of their staff to behaviour that is having an impact on the desired corporate culture.
+   for management to use the same norms and values in their staff dealings.

III   Coaching
+   for management to give their employees feedback and coaching in relation to their behaviour,
+   for management to give their staff on-the-job supervision where necessary,
−   for management to have too much work on their hands to coach their staff,
−   for management to leave it up to their staff to sort things out instead of coaching them.

IV   Dealing with change
+   for management to demonstrate the necessity for any announced changes,
−   to make changes without taking account of all the main factors,
+   or management to be clear about the effects of any announced changes,
+   for staff members who will be affected by changes to be involved in the process.

V   Showing appreciation
-   to only hear from management when things go wrong,
+   for management to also show its appreciation for a useful contribution (by giving a pat on a the shoulder, for example),
+   for management to recognize good work when it sees it and to show its appreciation (even for those things that are not the main focal point),
+   for management to give all due praise for exceptional achievements.

VI   Confrontation
+   for management to take action when things go wrong and to confront those concerned,
+   to be allowed to say "no" (even to management) if we really do not want something,
-   for conflicts to be avoided for the sake of peace and quiet,
-   for a blind eye to be turned and confrontation avoided when someone fails to meet his/her commitments.

VII Creativity and innovation
-   for people to be quick to say why something is *not* possible,
+   for people to encourage each other to find new ways and opportunities,
+   for people to look for ways of improving our products and work methods,
-   for people to want to hold on to the tried and true instead of trying out something new.

VIII Thinking a step ahead (long-term thinking)
-   for people to be constantly fighting problems rather than preventing them in the first place,
+   for people to think before they act,
-   for initiatives that do not have short-term results to be put on the back burner,
+   for problems not only to be resolved but for moves to be made to prevent them from occurring again.

IX	**Effectiveness**
+	for time, people and resources to be attuned to each other,
−	or there to be uncertainty about how one's contribution will be measured, appraised and evaluated,
+	to work to achieve results,
+	to carefully weigh up the benefits of a certain course of action against its cost.

X	**Tasks, responsibilities and competencies**
+	to know what one's tasks, responsibilities and competencies are,
+	for tasks, responsibilities and competencies to be attuned to each other,
+	for responsibilities and competencies to lie in areas that people are most skilled in,
−	for there to be an overlap of competencies or for them to be ignored.

XI	**Conscientiousness/discipline**
−	to turn a blind eye when someone forgets something or omits to do something,
+	to do a good job and to do it right now,
+	to meet one's commitments,
+	to finish what one has started.

XII	**Dealing with work pressure**
−	to try to get more out of others than one can reasonably expect,
+	for people to set boundaries and to say "no" if they know they will not be able to cope with the work coming their way,
−	to allow oneself the time to do one's work well,
−	to habitually take on more work than one can manage.

XIII	**Decisiveness**
−	to push decisions through, even in the face of resistance,
+	to make decisions in an efficient manner,
−	for decisions not to be acted on,
−	for decisions to be postponed.

XIV   Willingness to help/quality

−   to offer your services if you can get something out of it yourself,

+   to be courteous and attentive in providing the information that clients (both internal and external) want,

+   to always be prepared to help others,

+   to show enough interest in internal clients as to seek contact with them.

XV   Service provision

+   to think along with internal clients,

+   to set clear boundaries in complying (or not complying) with the wishes of internal clients,

−   for internal clients to dictate what we do without giving them permission to do so,

−   for it to be left up to the individual to decide which internal clients' demands/expectations to satisfy.

XVI   Cooperation between departments

−   for departments to ignore each other instead of cooperating,

+   to treat internal clients in the same way as one would treat external ones,

+   for departments to cooperate with each other if necessary and desirable,

−   to mainly look after one's own departmental turf.

XVII Team spirit/working cooperatively

+   for one's colleagues to listen to each other and to be open to each other,

+   to demonstrate team spirit in working together,

−   for it to be regarded as a sign of weakness if a colleague has a problem,

+   for colleagues to assist each other during busy times.

XVIII Entrepreneurial spirit
+   to take the time to experiment in order to get better results in the long run,
–   for risk-taking and making mistakes to be punished instead of being seen as part of the learning process,
–   to wait for opportunities to come one's way instead of taking the initiative,
+   to take the initiative with new things without being asked to do so.

XIX   Openness
–   to have to disguise criticism,
+   to be allowed to have one's say without fear of the consequences,
+   to be prepared to listen to critical questions and comments,
+   not to broadcast opinions that one might have of others.

XX   Information
–   to have to prize the information you need out of others,
+   to be aware of who needs what information,
–   for information from the shop floor to get lost in transit,
+   for information to be quickly relayed from the top down the bottom.

XXI   Communication
+   to listen carefully to others before reacting,
–   for people to talk *at* each other rather than *to* each other,
+   for people not only to give each other information but also to discuss things,
+   to allow a two-way flow during work discussions.

FROM REACTIVITY TO CREATIVITY

"Quick! Come and look at this! World War Three has broken out!" called out Huub's wife as she came rushing into the room. Guust, Huub and I looked at each other. We were in the middle of an interesting conversation about values within organizations.

"There's been an attack on the World Trade Center! A plane has smashed into it!"

Again we looked at each other, until one of us said, "Look, we can run over to the television and see what's going on, but if World War Three really has broken out there's nothing we can do about it. Shall we finish our discussion?" And so we went back to the topic. Instead of reacting by devouring television images, we decided to spend our time as we saw fit. In retrospect, I was pleased we had made this decision, because it gave rise to a good discussion that I would not like to have missed.

I had introduced Guust to Huub Kortehaas, whom I had got to know several months previously and whose sculptures had made a big impression on me. Most of his sculptures, which he exhibited in his own garden (or rather, his own park) expressed some value or another. I was secretly hoping that Guust would be as attracted to them as I was and would commission Huub to make one for Philip Morris Holland. I could see it in my mind's eye already.

We were sitting in Huub's studio. One enormous wall – 9.9 metres long and 3.3 metres high – was like a field filled with gilded budding plants. There were 99 of the 9 centimetre-high plants, each with the names of a well-known person and a letter from him or her. 33 of them came from the spiritual, artistic and philosophic "I" world, 33 came from the political, economic and executive "we" world (Gorbachov and Kurt Waldheim, for example) and 33 were from the world of science and research: the "it" world.

The budding plant was a metaphor for the potential human capacity for growth. Gold stood for spirituality. There was a photo of Huub standing side-by-side with Gorbachov in a corner of the same room. Huub described himself as an alchemist in search of a symbiosis between spirituality and the economy, between culture and nature, between Eastern and Western thinking, between the individual and society. It was an uplifting conversation. Too uplifting to be disturbed by the Third World War.

We finished our conversation three quarters of an hour later and then went and watched television. We saw a repeat of the second plane smashing into the tower just a few minutes prior to this. What we saw shocked us.

Our meeting was so much at odds with what we were witnessing. An extreme demonstration of fundamentalist values reeled past our eyes: utter destructiveness, utter reactivity, the ultimate in personal commitment, with the hijackers prepared to offer up their own lives for the sake of what we could only see as a religious matter, beyond our understanding as Westerners. Or was it?

Organizations require people to be totally dedicated and committed to achieving the company's goals, even pushing them past the limit sometimes. Organizations expect their employees to share their view and their mission and they set a premium on loyalty and dedication. They expect people to conform to their organizational norms or to leave. There is not much difference between fanaticism and enthusiasm: the former is taking a good thing too far, or in other words, too much of the latter. In this respect, Al-Qaeda is not fundamentally different from most organizations. You could even quibble about whether terrorism is reactive or creative in nature. Terrorists will view the way they act in terms of creating a new world. They will refer to deeds of self-sacrifice, not suicide missions. In their eyes, their deeds are much the same as the heroic deeds we admire in our war heroes: their willingness to sacrifice themselves for a noble goal. What is the difference?

It is mainly in the degree of *inclusiveness* as against *exclusiveness*. To be inclusive is not to eliminate one's opponent but to obtain back-up. Inclusiveness has no "anti" and no antagonist. If there is, the result will be reactivity, trouble, destructiveness and destruction. The Other – the enemy – must be destroyed: there is no place for him or her in a world that belongs to us. Whether it be an armed combat or competitors battling it out, the issue is whether the other may exist too (inclusiveness) or not (exclusiveness).

The path to greater inclusiveness is the organic path, one whereby the "it" world does not preclude the "we" and the "I" worlds, in which the "we" world embraces the "it" and the "I" worlds, and the "I" world opens itself up to the "it" and the "we" worlds. Science ("it"), ethics ("we") and spirituality ("I") are worlds which belong inseparably together. Lasting solutions depend on bringing them all together instead of excluding one or more. Leadership is the linchpin.

We will only be able to transform reactive organizations into creative ones when each and every individual has learned the art of seeing the world through three sets of eyes.

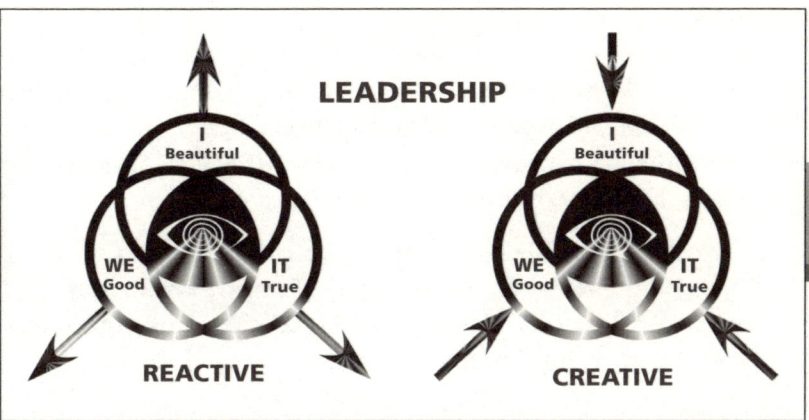

The words "reactivity" and "creativity" are actually anagrams. Do we have the art to pluck the "c" from the middle of "reactivity" and put it in front?

So the same, but all so different,
So far away, but so close to me,
So hard to do, but now so easy,
Once in a trap, but now so free.

So together, but so lonely,
So united, but not with you.
Give me, please, the skill to do it,
To love myself, and my enemy too.

Can we take that "c" and change our tune?
On my heart I make this vow,
when I've finally worked it out,
I'll come along and tell you how.

SOURCES

The Core Quadrant Theory is described in the book *Core Qualities: a Gateway to Human Resources* by Daniel Ofman, Scriptum Publishers, Schiedam, the Netherlands, ISBN 90 5594 240 5. This book is also available in Dutch, Danish, German and Russian.

The *Core Quadrant Game* is a card game that allows you to become acquainted with the Core Quadrant in a light-hearted way. Published by Core Quality Pty Ltd, Bussum, the Netherlands. This game is also available in Dutch and German.

The relationship between core qualities and the Enneagram is the subject of the book *The Core Qualities of the Enneagram* by Daniel Ofman and Rita van der Weck. Published by Scriptum Publishers, the Netherlands, ISBN 90 5594 244 8. This book is also available in Dutch.

The CD-ROMs *Core Qualities and the Core Quadrant,* and *The Core Qualities of the Enneagram,* both by Daniel Ofman, are also available (also in Dutch).

Three CD-ROMs that treat the relationship between the Enneagram and core qualities are also available.
All these products are available via book shops or Core Quality's Web-based shop www.corequality.nl.

Core Quality Pty Ltd
Lindelaan 14A
1405 AK Bussum
The Netherlands
Tel.: (+31) 35 691 29 30
Fax: (+31) 35 692 26 26
E-mail: daniel@ofman.nl
Website: www.corequality.nl

Kernkwadrant® (Core Quadrant) is a registered trade mark of Core Quality Pty Ltd.